FORSYTH LIBRARY - FHSU
378.1554K 736 1969
Kniz...
2 1765 0008 0348

Higher
Adult Education
in the United States

Higher Adult Education in the United States

The Current Picture, Trends, and Issues

By Malcolm S. Knowles

Prepared for the Committee on Higher Adult Education
American Council on Education
Washington, D.C.

COMMITTEE ON
HIGHER ADULT EDUCATION

Sponsored by Commission on Academic Affairs

For the Commission on Academic Affairs

DEAN WALLACE COLVARD, *Chairman;* Chancellor, University of North Carolina at Charlotte

THURMAN J. WHITE, Dean, University Extension, University of Oklahoma

PAUL C. REINERT, S. J., President, Saint Louis University

Representing Organizations

American Association of Junior Colleges: OSCAR H. EDINGER, JR., President of Mount San Antonio College

Association for Field Services in Teacher Education: CHARLES LONGACRE, President; Director of Extension, Newark State College

Association of University Evening Colleges: ERNEST E. MCMAHON, President; Dean, University Extension, Rutgers—The State University

National Association of State Universities and Land-Grant Colleges (Cooperative Extension Section): JOHN B. CLAAR, Director, Cooperative Extension Service, College of Agriculture, University of Illinois

National University Extension Association: STANLEY C. ROBINSON, President; Director of Continuing Education, University of Illinois

Members at Large

JOHN B. HOLDEN, Director, Graduate School, U. S. Department of Agriculture

CYRIL O. HOULE, Professor of Education, University of Chicago

ASA S. KNOWLES, President, Northeastern University

DONALD R. MCNEIL, Chancellor, University Extension, University of Wisconsin

---

Committee membership, as of October 31, 1968, when publication of the Knowles study was approved.

378.1554
K73h
1969

© 1969 by the AMERICAN COUNCIL ON EDUCATION
One Dupont Circle, Washington, D.C. 20036
Library of Congress Catalog Card No. 70–92269

Second Impression, March 1970

Printed in the United States of America. SBN 8268–1317–8

Foreword

I think it was Stephen Leacock who once noted education's tendency "to eat up life." He made his observation more than a generation ago when graduation from high school or college often marked the end of formal schooling. One wonders what he might say now if he read this present study and sensed the wide range and extended time span of the activities it sets forth. Would he not have to agree that continuing education sustains rather than consumes human life?

This truism is well recognized by leaders in the field of higher adult education—a field of endeavor, incidentally, that is not clearly delineated in the minds of the thousands of persons who participate in it. In an effort to clarify matters, a group of leaders came together more than four years ago to launch a comprehensive study. The American Council on Education agreed to sponsor it.

Back in 1965 it looked as if a year or so might suffice for the survey. Changes in committee membership and in Council staff were not anticipated, however, and it was only a few months ago that the fact-gathering and writing were completed.

Because of the growing importance of higher adult education, the appearance of this publication will, I am sure, be welcomed on many sides. Not only does it survey the current scene, but also it points up trends and issues. All who read it will doubtless feel indebted to those whose efforts should enhance our general understanding and appreciation of the real significance of the subject of this study.

Logan Wilson, *President*
American Council on Education

v

Preface

Midpoint in the decade of the sixties it was clear, if it had not been before, that education was regarded by large segments of the American populace as a lifelong process. Many institutions, agencies, and corporations were sponsoring educational programs, some bestowing academic credit and some operating on a noncredit basis, to serve individuals and groups of people of all ages in almost every geographic region. Following World War II, and concurrent with the technological revolution which ensued, the mastery of mind over matter required education and training as never before. Although historically the sponsorship of extension education by the United States government had been limited largely to the Department of Agriculture, by the mid-sixties many governmental agencies were underwriting, either directly or through cooperating institutions, some sort of extension or adult education program. It was inevitable that the felt need for more coordination and clarity would stimulate leaders to joint actions in this field.

The Committee on Higher Adult Education of the American Council on Education had its beginning in a meeting of about twenty-five adult education leaders in Boston, Massachusetts, on March 12, 1965. Discussions focused on the need for coordination in dealing with issues that were national in scope. The Reverend Richard T. Deters, chairman, Advisory Committee of the Association of University Evening Colleges, presided. Present were representatives of the Adult Education Association of the U.S.A., American Association of Junior Colleges, American Council on Education, Association for Field Services in Teacher Education, National Association of State Universities and Land-Grant Colleges, Canadian Association of Directors of Extension and Summer School, Center for the Study of Liberal Education for Adults at Boston University, Council of Graduate Schools in the United States, Evening Student Personnel Association, and National University Extension Association. The deliberations of this group generated a request to the American Council on Education that it provide the leadership to bring about more coordination and also provide a medium for considering current and future issues in this field.

When the Council's Commission on Academic Affairs met at the University of Chicago on April 11–12, this matter was discussed and interest expressed. At a follow-up meeting on June 10, nine individuals representing organizations involved in higher adult education agreed that (1) the leadership of ACE in moving toward coordination in the field was highly desirable; (2) the ACE Commission on Academic Affairs should name an ad hoc committee to bring together a carefully selected group of delegates to outline a set of objectives for a coordinated program; (3) the committee would explore action the Council might take in the field of adult education; (4) the committee could help to clear up concepts and terminology in the field and possibly survey the scope of the enterprise; and (5) the committee could be established and a conference called in the fall of 1965.

When ACE held its Annual Meeting in Washington on October 7, the chairman of the Commission on Academic Affairs arranged a meeting for November 29 to determine the membership of the ad hoc committee. This committee was to comprise representatives of the following organizations: Association of University Evening Colleges, National University Extension Association, American Association of Junior Colleges, National Association of State Universities and Land-Grant Colleges (Cooperative Extension Section), and Association for Field Services in Teacher Education. Resource persons invited included Cyril O. Houle, professor of education, University of Chicago; Asa S. Knowles, president, Northeastern University; Malcolm Knowles, professor of education, Boston University; E. A. Liveright, director, Center for the Study of Liberal Education for Adults; Paul A. Miller, president, West Virginia University; William P. Tolley, chancellor, Syracuse University; and Talman W. Van Arsdale, Jr., president, Bradley University.

The ad hoc committee, convened on November 29 as planned, requested that ACE establish a standing committee on higher adult education under the aegis of the Commission on Academic Affairs. It also recommended that the committee join with the five organizations represented in its membership "in finding a man capable of making a study of higher adult education and its problems, and of providing general leadership in the move toward coordination." The Honorable Francis Keppel, then United States Commissioner of Education, was present and participated in the discussions.

President Logan Wilson of ACE followed through with the appointment of the standing committee and designated Paul A. Miller, president of West Virginia University, as the chairman. At its first meeting on April 20, 1966, the newly constituted Committee on Higher Adult Education agreed to sponsor a situation report that would (1) list and analyze recent and ongoing studies in higher adult education and (2) identify the major issues confronting this area of education. ACE agreed to underwrite a budget to support the situation report, and steps were taken to provide inputs for it. Robert J. Pitchell, executive director, National University Extension Association, agreed to prepare a paper to initiate this effort.

Soon after this first meeting Dr. Miller was appointed Assistant Secretary for Education, Department of Health, Education, and Welfare, and found it necessary to relinquish the chairmanship of the committee. It was at about this time that ACE appointed a new director of its Commission on Academic Affairs, Edward Joseph Shoben, Jr. With the appointment of the writer as chairman of the committee, plans were laid to activate the suggestion that had been adopted.

Following a review of Dr. Pitchell's report in late 1966, the committee decided to extend the analysis toward a publication that would deal with an overview of higher adult education in the United States and asked Malcolm S. Knowles to prepare it. Other members of the committee, including Dr. Houle and Donald R. McNeil, chancellor, University Extension, University of Wisconsin, agreed to submit statements to Dr. Knowles which might be used with Dr. Pitchell's contribution in preparation of the new report.

In spite of changes in the membership of the committee and in the staff of the Council, the committee continued its work, including the review of drafts of the report by Dr. Knowles. At a meeting on October 31, 1968, the committee, in cooperation with Dr. Wilson and Charles G. Dobbins, executive secretary of ACE, reviewed Dr. Knowles' final report entitled "Higher Adult Education in the United States—The Current Picture, Trends, and Issues." The committee recommended early publication and also asked Dr. Miller, currently professor of education at the University of North Carolina at Charlotte, to comment about the relevance of higher adult education in an introduction.

The Committee on Higher Adult Education is pleased to join with the American Council on Education in presenting the situation report by Dr. Knowles and the introductory essay by Dr. Miller. Appreciation is expressed to both authors, to others who contributed to the writing, and to the Council for its support. A special note of thanks is expressed to Mr. Dobbins for helping to bring the committee into being and then maintaining continuity during several changes in the personnel of the committee and the Council.

As chairman, I express my appreciation to other members of the committee and the organizations they represent. It is hoped that this publication will be useful both to institutions engaged in higher adult education and to those otherwise concerned with providing learning opportunities for all people throughout life. The publication of this report should be considered not as an end, but rather as a continuation of efforts toward clarity and coordination.

DEAN WALLACE COLVARD, *Chancellor*
University of North Carolina at Charlotte

Chairman, Committee on Higher Adult Education
American Council on Education
January 1969

Contents

... Moving from the Wings
An Introduction
by Paul A. Miller

Malcolm S. Knowles' timely review of higher adult education has about it the quality of the bench mark. After decades of working invisibly in the wings of higher education, adult learning is now burgeoning on every side. It has become recognized almost overnight as a distinct field of study and practice. New journals about adult education are being formed, international conferences are being held. A host of new federal laws depend to some degree upon adult education, and academic and other professional people toil with marked success at developing more useful theory and more rigorous methodology.

To be sure, there are many aspects of adult education, a field that has always been difficult to describe, that need much more thought. One of these, the subject of these remarks, is the implications of adult education for the expanding linkages between the university and the larger community. Dr. Knowles speaks of this, one of many reasons why his overview is so timely.

To begin with, there is a history of uncertainty in the American university about just what adult education is supposed to do. Given the overall purposes of the university, adult education, until recently, was as misunderstood as it was obvious. It has often appeared to be a separate activity, somewhat off the beaten track. However, in the past ten years, as change has brought devastating challenges to human competence, educators generally have advanced the theme that continuous learning is a necessary part of life. That the university should help people continue to learn has grown increasingly obvious. Nothing could seem more straightforward!

However, these straightforward beliefs have not been easy to convert into practice. There is a hybrid character about higher adult education, conceived as it was by several domestic and international parents. Adult education is not exclusively the offspring of education: social agencies, libraries, voluntary associations, churches, and government departments were all involved. Projects in adult education are as varied as the people who participate in them and who, on the whole, pay for them. Fortunately, these hybrid traditions have given adult education a healthy measure of hybrid vigor. It is a fascinating story from the annals of education that adult programs now draw upon this vigor as they flourish among the trademarks of postindustrial life. And they are doing so even as they are not fully understood.

It is just now that the importance of adult education is growing in those institutions of higher learning which formerly found difficulty in finding a place for it. Part of this new acceptance suggests the epochal passage of education over some great divide of social experience. Tumbling from that divide, the continuities of history seem scrambled, elusive, and sometimes less than useful. To change skills and attitudes continuously has become as relentlessly important as acquiring them initially. Education in general is expanding in every direction and turning into a concept of human resource development. Therefore, it is becoming less the province of the young; it is moving from the learning space of the classroom to that of the community.

This is not to say, however, that continuous adult learning for a lifetime is given the attention that it deserves. The colleges and universities are especially neglectful, although some have taken enormous steps to advance the field. While the very meaning of education is adapting to new requirements of human growth and development, the institutional structure of higher education still lags behind. Colleges and universities fail to link up very well with the lower schools and this failure adds discontinuity. Teachers at all levels lose sight of their students and normally are unaware of how much in their own experience they managed to keep on learning. It is an unusual senate agenda in the academic precinct that includes items of concern about what educational goals are possible once formal instruction is completed.

Looking across the vast front of American education, one finds a spectacular growth of adult education in its many forms, yet also a sustained uncertainty about how best to fit it into overall institutional goals. One reason for this uncertainty is that adult educators have not always been in position to define and to testify on behalf of the relationship adult education bears to institutional aims. A true profession for adult educators did not exist until recently. People came to adult education from other tasks, sometimes by default, without related preparation or clear choice among career options. Only recently has the field made claim to a body of theory and practice. And, in much of higher education at least, programs of adult learning have been sponsored only as they were able to pay their own way.

Dr. Knowles describes several aspects of adult education in the American mode, especially as they have been sponsored by colleges and universities. All of them have known the frustration of being unheard by the councils of authority in university life. This oversight, and sometimes plain neglect, in the past has led to some consequences which further planning must now take into account.

First, higher adult education has not been acknowledged as perhaps the most consciously planned linkage of the university with the community.

During a period when institutions have increased their concern with off-campus activities, normally the rule has not been to recognize that the longstanding traditions of adult education have much to say about additional ties between the academy and society. Since contemporary society likely will demand still more assistance from higher education, institutions will be tempted to respond directly and quickly to urgent claims rather than to carefully planned objectives.

Second, extensive confusion still exists about the meaning of higher adult education: is it education, service, or public relations? This confusion nurtures the belief that teaching on campus is an academic function while teaching off campus is a service function. Whenever this distinction emerges, the status of adult education is likely to be depressed. Faculty rewards for time and interest in adult education then tend to decline, and the idea that learning in one place is somehow more legitimate than in another is reinforced.

Third, adult educators have more knowledge of the interests of adults than they have been able to persuade their institutions to use. The emphasis by adults on problems rather than subject matter makes it difficult for universities to know how to organize an appropriate response. The temptation to do the same thing for adults as for younger students may win favor with the faculty, but normally it misses the mark with older people desirous of continuing their education. When plans are made in response to the needs and desires of adult learners, the lack of faculty interest may reduce the prestige of adult education.

Fourth, program planning on higher adult education has been studied too little for an assessment of its importance vis-à-vis present challenges. For example, urgent demands for the assignment of resources to urban society may induce higher education to respond as the physician for community pathologies. A more assured contribution would result from deliberate planning, setting priorities, and projecting, testing, and evaluating projects. More of these skills, part of the capital of adult education, should be shared with higher education.

Although adult education programs are growing by leaps and bounds, there is a persistent reluctance to fit them into the main body of educational activity. Nowhere is this reluctance more evident than in the American college and university. Some of the reasons are easily understood. First of all, adult learning is normally an activity that consumes but part of the student's time and frequently only part of the teacher's time. As schooling became separated from family and community life, sharper distinctions were made between students and workers. And, until the social order began to change so swiftly, it could be assumed that much of what was learned as a youth would be useful for a lifetime.

A second important reason for difficulty in incorporating the idea of part-time learning into the main body of full-time practice is that, more than other functions of the university, adult education must take into account not only the student's hopes but also the nature of the social or professional group to which he belongs. Adult education projects cannot be confined to the classroom or conference center because they almost always bear upon the aspirations of individuals and the jurisdictions of groups. These complexities do not make of adult programs something that is less than education. But such programs must be developed along lines which suggest that, even as individuals may be educationally advanced by them, the community welfare as a whole must in some fashion also be enhanced. In addition, as the connection between higher adult education and effective social institutions becomes clearer, it is even more necessary for adult educators to chart the ways by which the field may contribute to the public good. This task, growing in importance as higher adult education moves from the wings, may be considered as follows:

Basic Citizenship. One may sense a rise of doubt that education is able to do what it proposes. The utilities of education remain as confused as they are celebrated. Little more than a taste of learning in poor countries can turn revolutions of rising hopes into still other revolutions of rising demands. On the other hand, education in the advanced countries seems a puny instrument indeed when it confronts the decline of social and environmental quality. Domestic violence and international conflict provide no certainty that education as it is known is correlated with human sentiment. And in the United States, education seems uncertain about itself, its future, its students, its ethical structure, and its usefulness to society. Possibly education is undergoing a substantial crisis of efficacy.

The army of people who give themselves to the tasks of education must now be asked if they have done enough to cultivate the values of fundamental citizenship. No part of the world seems excused from taking another look at the underlying aspects of citizenship—those responsibilities and satisfactions of living in the family, the community, one's country, and the world community. The continuities of history and tradition seem most scrambled when occupation is separated from family and community life, when the work ethic elevates the prestige of occupation, and family and community tasks are thrown back upon themselves for invention.

Adult educators always rise to special eloquence when the topic becomes education for public responsibility. Their greatest essays portray the cultivated citizen who learns continuously. Perhaps it is an emphasis that enables adult educators to be certain that human performance can grow and improve as it continues. Public affairs, world affairs, family life—all are phrases that adult educators have clung to for a long time. The same is true of community development: for all its many forms, adult educators have never given it up as one basic way to create the learning community. That all these approaches to education for basic citizenship are not more numerous and acceptable stems from haphazard financing and from the underlying American appetite for vocational training.

Enriching the practice of basic citizenship will undoubtedly occupy higher adult education for the balance of the twentieth century. More attention must be given to how undergraduate instruction may prepare the student to understand and accept the need of continued learning for humane pursuits as much as for avowedly vocational ones. The adult educator will be required to understand education as a whole. He will have to advocate learning that makes little distinction between youth and adults, an education for a basic citizenship which calls for the language of brotherhood. He will need to advance a universal education, as useful to intercultural understanding in the world as it is to intercultural understanding in the inner city. Such hopes are not likely to be realized without the concerted support of universities on the side of the helping professions. University adult education must be regarded as among their most effective instruments.

The Urban Strategy. In any review of its course as a contributor to the public welfare, higher adult education is bound up with the search for a strategy of urban development. Americans want to remake their cities while simultaneously seeking more immediate solutions to the critical issues in education, job training, housing, and health care. No single institution can do much alone. Every level of government is necessary, as well as are common goals among private and public bodies, new types of community services, and still more knowledge and talent. Higher education finds itself at the heart of the urban action, yet less than certain about what it properly should do. Meanwhile, the urgency grows daily for higher education to make up its mind.

The fragmentation of urban life accounts for many dilemmas: few surpass the wastage of information—data that are produced only to miss delivery for use at the right time. Individual communities fail to up-date experience, and there is too little sharing of experience among them. Since it stores and enlarges the human record, the university serves more than any other institution as the memory of society. The importance of this function has grown enormously. More information must be delivered more quickly; the interdependence in knowledge must be portrayed; the data must be disseminated in a manner to reveal old needs and impart new ones. It is useful to recall that the land-grant university remained at the heart of the rural revolution because it devised and held the central position in a national network of communication. Whether the university can conduct itself similarly in the urban society is still far from clear.

The institutes and other structures of higher adult education are aligned with both the university and the community. In recent ventures, such as the chain of state-wide councils under Title I of the Higher Education Act, ways have been found to merge local projects into a national system for identifying conditions that are amenable to improvement by the application of research and education. Moreover, the achievements of the agricultural extension services are only partially understood as they may relate to the urban task. These extension services have an important part to play in the new regional communities that are neither uniquely rural nor urban.

The Professions. Contemporary society is characterized by the shift from manual occupations to professional services. This trend will not abate. Accordingly, the essential quality of life comes increasingly to depend upon the performance of professional people. Whether they function in the private or public sectors, professional practitioners feel, more than any other group, the mounting pressure of having to discard old ideas and learn new ways. To help them adapt to this pressure is an expanding obligation of universities and of adult education in particular.

These pressures not only strike the practitioner, they also influence his profession as a whole—from medicine and public accountancy to politics. It is both impossible and unethical for any profession to ignore procedures for elevating performance. Since continuous learning is indigenous to the meaning of profession, it can never be casual. Indeed, continuous learning is part of professional practice itself. Higher adult education has no more visible task than to continue professional education. And it is unlikely that any task will bring such enthusiastic response and approval.

However, as is occurring in so many other fields, distinctions between preservice and continuing education are fading away. The formal preparation before practice can include only a small and declining part of the knowledge of a specific professional field. As a result, there are widespread upheavals throughout preservice education for professional practice. The strain could be reduced if institutions, adult educators, and professional societies could gain a cooperative perspective of education as a lifelong process. While much is being done, continuing professional education offers most colleges and universities their best chance to strengthen ties with the larger community.

In many respects the best performance of higher adult education across the years has been in upgrading occupational and professional skills. More than many of their colleagues, adult educators observed the shift to services which was taking place and recognized that these services could not be performed excellently for the client without the belief in lifelong learning. It may be recalled also that adult education has had coordinate experiences: a concern for volunteer talent and the need for new forms of the helping professions. Meanwhile, a new chapter of continuing education is opening up. It reveals the ethical horizons of professional practice which lie beyond the acquisition of knowledge. In the process of continued learning, professional judgment cannot be fed by data alone.

New Arrangements. As lifelong learning becomes more acceptable and practiced in the general culture, new instruments and institutions will be in order. The fusing of urban communities into vast aggregations of population raises the question of where people will go to find nearby centers for further education. The recent experimentation with various kinds of neighborhood centers indicates that better ways of mingling neighborhood services will be found. It would be surprising if urban schools did not enlarge the scope of their activities to make them more helpful to adults.

The same is true of higher education, given recently to experimentation with new types of colleges. There is hope that this trend, together with concern for human deprivation, will forge a new arrangement that might well be called Samaritan College, one that would reveal ways to reach the poor, teach the infirm, and encompass the needs of the wounded. By some additional leap of adult education, perhaps new kinds of learning centers for adults will spring up dedicated to the reduction of "lostness," to the method of seeking, and to the joy of human fulfillment.

The problem of mastering the uses of telecommunications is of the same order. The modern community is ready for learning by new media and for a definition of the learning space no less extensive than the technical limits of electronic communication. Institutional systems for using the computer and television in ways that would connect individual communities with many centers of competence are now possible. This is a job for academic men, including those adult educators who have gained experience with some of the vexing problems: how to balance individual and group interests; how to join education with industry and government; how to employ the media to increase citizen participation. These questions not only belong on the work lists of higher education; they should also move up in the priorities of adult programs.

The Conversant Patron. In the interest of balancing competitive aims, it is customary to speak of university functions as teaching, research, and public service. Unfortunately, these are so general as to be misleading for discussions among academic scholars and patrons. They do not, for example, express those deep-felt and specific goals of the scholarly community—academic freedom and the canons of excellence—which lie beneath most acts of teaching and research. This is among the reasons why laymen on the whole are less conversant with the history and the reasoning back of these deeper goals.

How more and more college graduates may continue to discuss

educational goals in sophisticated terms is a large question before higher education in the United States and elsewhere. It rises at a time when the usual practice is to convert alumni into quite special constituencies. To politicize alumni into groups or lobbies for advancing the fortunes of particular institutions is by no means unheard of. While institution-building frequently may require such pragmatic techniques, they are troublesome in a day when enormous requests for public support are in need of constituencies whose loyalties go much beyond the fortunes of specific institutions.

The pivotal importance of universities in a society organized around the use of knowledge would seem to require forums that go far beyond the whimsical creation of special constituencies. Laymen need to confront the deeper academic goals in a more continuing and penetrating manner. Scholars need to show more interest in reconciling educational resources with public hopes and despairs. Helping to establish such discussions, and finding ways to keep them going, is important business for higher adult education. Such ventures as the alumni colleges may point the way. But whatever the technique, the enlisted patron will advance the humanization of institutions as he joins with scholars in widening the basis of informed discussion about university life.

Dr. Knowles, devoted servant and leader of adult education, shares his overview of a field that normally defies digestion. His summary is succinct, moving across the traditions of adult education, outlining its present trends, and saying a good deal about its problems and promises. His is a report that will prove useful to academic administrators who frequently have difficulty in tracking down the many forms of higher adult education. The document should also interest those faculty planning committees whose members feel more at home with aims that center on the campus than with those whose motif may be shaped off the campus.

Continuous adult learning is rising in the order of academic goods. The number of adult learners, when added to those who have entered vocational training, is as large as the number of students formally enrolled in schools and colleges. This widespread adult group, drawn from every walk and profession of life, makes the reference to the United States as a learning society much more than rhetoric. The problem of coping with the enormity of this idea is before every policy council at every level of American education.

It is heartening that the American Council on Education found it possible to sponsor the overview of higher adult education by Dr. Knowles. While adult education grew up with something less than perfect design and understanding, it is now lusty enough to merit national attention in policy planning. In addition, notwithstanding the practical American view of education, it is not too much to ask that the country know more about the relation of continuous learning to the humane vocations, how these vocations may be preserved and, here and there, how they may be restored.

University of North Carolina at Charlotte
and North Carolina State University at Raleigh

Higher
Adult Education
in the United States

1 Why This Study?

American higher education is in transition as regards its role, its structure, its size, its methods, its program, its basis of support, and its relationship with its constituencies. About this fact of contemporary life the social analysts have no doubts.

An increasing number of voices are being raised to identify this happening, however, not as transition but as *revolution*—the radical change in the basic character of the university from an institution primarily serving youth to one serving at least equally adults and community.

For example, two voices from a special issue of *Daedalus, Toward the Year 2000: Work in Progress:*

The present university population mix—overwhelmingly undergraduate and predoctoral or preprofessional—will change dramatically in the next thirty-five years, at least in university cities. There, great numbers of post-doctoral fellows and professional adults of all ages will congregate for longer or shorter periods. They will be seeking something quite different from what is today so quaintly called "continuing education." Long before the year 2000, a businessman will be as apt to spend a sabbatical year at a university as in travel and sport. When men and women no longer deem it unreasonable to pursue two or three different careers in succession, the university city will provide the stimulus (and the instruction) to make such things possible.[1]

The changes in our intellectual institutions that will work themselves out over the next thirty-three years are not merely modifications within existing organizations . . . , but more fundamental developments that will generate new and transform old institutional forms. The universities, for example, are under multiple pressures for change caused by the side-effects of federal support, the demands of regional and community development, the creation of cross-disciplinary centers, the fading boundaries between training and work, and the demands from the new society of the young. As a result, a variety of new organizational forms linked more closely to community needs, to work, and to living currents of industrial-political-intellectual life than to the traditional community of scholars will be developed within, outside, and beside the campus.[2]

From the Carnegie Foundation for the Advancement of Teaching:

What would appear to be desirable now, where needed, is the modernization of the university's governance to take account of all three functions in which the typical institution is engaged today—teaching, research, *and* public service. Such a process would have the salutary effect of focusing the entire

1. Stephen R. Graubard, "University Cities in the Year 2000," *Daedalus* 96 (Summer 1967): 820.
2. Harold Orlans, "Educational and Scientific Institutions," *Daedalus* 96 (Summer 1967): 830.

3

academic community's thought on the function of public service and perhaps lead to a redefinition of the meaning of the university in today's world. It would at the very least bring to many people the realization that the governance of universities is becoming a matter of far more than institutional significance—that it relates directly to the viability of our knowledge-centered society.[3]

From the chancellor of Syracuse University:

Of all the forces at work in the shaping of our new idea of the American university, few have had so profound or pervasive an effect as adult or continuing education. Considered only a few decades ago to be a peripheral activity of the university, concerned primarily with the administration of educational programmes for farmers and housewives at the high school level, adult education has emerged since the war as one of the significant and urgent missions of the modern university.[4]

From *The College Student and His Culture:*

In view of (a) the increasing market for continuing education caused by the increase in our older population (both in numbers and proportionally), (b) the rising need for continuing education growing out of the increasing complexity in our life and in the decisions we must make, and (c) the greater opportunities for participation in continuing education stemming from the growth of leisure time, the following imperatives become apparent: (1) The resources for, and the availability of, adult education should be greatly increased without delay; the need is a real and growing one. (2) New forms, structures, and institutional arrangements for adult education are required; these new institutional forms and creations should make better use of new technical and physical developments, especially in the field of communication. (3) Education for adults perhaps should increasingly concern itself with values and attitudes as opposed to simple skills, facts, and information. This area of ethics has long been neglected, but a truly educated and learned society cannot permit this to continue. (4) Adult education must increasingly become a way of life, rather than a luxury for those who can afford it. The federal government undoubtedly will lend greater financial assistance to adult education programs than it has in the past so that disadvantaged persons can also be involved. (5) Administrators and programmers in the field have to devise and utilize new methods for recruiting, motivating, and retaining prospective adult learners. (6) Leaders in the field of adult higher education must become more concerned about widening their audiences so they involve not only the elite, but also the man-in-the-street.[5]

The problem appears to be, essentially, cultural lag: the constituency of the university has been shifting toward the adult end of the spectrum while the service of the university has been shifting toward the larger community. The governance and policy structure remain much the same as when the university's constituency was primarily youth, and its program orientation remains much the same as when services were primarily teaching and research.

3. "The University at the Service of Society," 1966–67 *Annual Report* (New York: Carnegie Foundation for the Advancement of Teaching, 1967), p. 13.
4. Tolley, 1967, p. 15.
5. Kaoru Yamamoto, ed., *The College Student and His Culture: An Analysis* (Boston: Houghton Mifflin Co., 1968), pp. 487–88.

The concept of learning as a lifelong process has emerged as one of the explosive ideas of the second half of the twentieth century. Colleges and universities are experiencing enormous pressures to clarify, if not to revise, their role, policies, and program in the continuing education of adults. The policy makers and faculties of institutions of higher education, therefore, desperately need help in confronting issues that, once peripheral, are now central.

THE PURPOSE OF THIS STUDY

This study was originally commissioned by the Committee on Higher Adult Education of the American Council on Education to serve its own need for a condensed but comprehensive assessment of the current situation vis-à-vis the education of adults in our institutions of higher education. In order to make responsible recommendations to the Council concerning this dimension of higher education, the committee needed an overview of the current picture, trends, and issues as revealed in the literature of the field.

But as the committee examined the first draft of the report, the idea evolved that an overview of this sort might be useful to the administrators and faculty members of institutions of higher education, to people in government who have responsibilities for governmental policies affecting higher adult education, and to citizens who are concerned with this area of educational service. The report, therefore, was revised with this larger audience in mind.

The purpose of this study, then, is to provide a guide to discussion and inquiry. It does not profess to provide a platform or blueprint for the future, but to identify problems that need solutions and issues that need confrontation. The author hopes that it will stimulate leaders of higher education, both nationally and within individual institutions, to initiate strategies for involving all relevant parties in solving these problems and confronting these issues. In the last analysis, the purpose of this study is to launch a higher adult educational process.

THE METHODOLOGY

Although this study was conducted by a single investigator, and he must take final responsibility for its results, it is the product of the efforts of many people.

The basic design was adapted from an outline provided by Cyril O. Houle, professor of education at the University of Chicago. Extensive informal memoranda considering contemporary issues were provided by Donald R. McNeil, chancellor, University Extension, University of Wisconsin; and Robert J. Pitchell, executive director, National University Extension Association. Detailed suggestions for the revision of the first draft were submitted by Oscar H. Edinger, Jr., president, Mt. San Antonio College, Walnut, California; Cyril O. Houle; Ernest E. McMahon, dean, University Extension Division, Rutgers University–The State University of New Jersey; Stanley C. Robinson, dean of extension, University of Illinois, and president of the NUEA—all members of the Committee on Higher Adult Education—and Kenneth D. Roose, vice-president of the American Council on Education.

The basic methodology of this study was a content analysis of abstracts of over 170 books, monographs, and papers provided by the ERIC Clearinghouse on Adult Education and the Library of Continuing Education at Syracuse University under the direction of Roger DeCrow. This collection of abstracts of major writings about higher adult education since 1960, reproduced in the bibliography, exemplifies the enormous value of the recently established ERIC Clearinghouse to scholars in this field. It also illustrates that, while little attention has been paid to adult education in the general literature of higher education, a substantial body of literature on higher adult education has been developing separately.

This study, then, is essentially an analysis of the literature of higher adult education from 1960 through 1968, as documented by ERIC. No attempt was made to collect information beyond these sources, since it is believed that they best represent the state of the field as now known. A few documents published prior to 1960 have been used because of their historical significance, and some documents not appearing in the ERIC bibliography have been cited for special purposes.

Sources of statements made in the study are identified by footnotes at the end of each chapter; most of the references are listed in the bibliography. These references do not necessarily indicate agreement by the authors with the points of view expressed in the statements but only that their writings contain information about the statements.

Some difficulty was encountered in terminology in this complex field, and, in the interest of simplicity and space, *university* is frequently used to include all institutions of higher education and *extension* is used to include all types of adult education.

THE ORGANIZATION

The analysis of the literature of higher adult education starts with an attempt to place the field in perspective. Chapter 2 presents a brief synopsis of the historical roots and a broad-stroke picture of the current situation. Chapter 3 identifies some of the external and internal forces that seem to be pressing for change. Chapter 4 summarizes the trends discerned in the literature, and chapter 5 isolates the national, state, and institutional issues that are revealed as concerns of adult educators in institutions of higher education.

Appendix A reorganizes these issues into a classification system to serve as a guide to policy makers in constructing guidelines to policy and practice for the field and for their institutions. Appendix B suggests some operational objectives and questions as a starting point for evaluating existing institutional programs. Appendix C presents a general set of guidelines promulgated by the NUEA which might serve as another framework for the development of more specific guidelines by individual institutions.

SOME PERSONAL THOUGHTS ON THE USE OF THIS STUDY

The author's impression, as a result of immersion in the literature during this study, is that what is most needed is the clarification of appropriate guidelines to policy and practice in higher adult education.

Most of the issues identified in the last section of the study exist largely because there are no commonly accepted yardsticks against which institutions can measure their policies and practices. This is much like the situation that existed in the field of medical education before the Flexner report. And perhaps, as in that case, once the yardsticks become available, the issues will start to be resolved. Many other examples of the utility of guidelines could be cited in such diverse aspects of higher education as college admissions, accreditation, social work education, professional preparation of educational administrators, and so on.

Guidelines of this sort can be created in a variety of ways. They can be promulgated by an individual (as with Flexner) or by the leaders of the institutional grouping involved (as with the Council on Social Work Education) or by a coalition of relevant elements of the higher educational enterprise.

The author could visualize many benefits from action on the part of the Committee on Higher Adult Education in constructing a set of guidelines, perhaps having them pretested by a sampling of institutions and the leadership of the relevant professional associations, and then inviting institutions across the country to use them as the basis for a process of self-assessment with results to be pooled, analyzed, and published.

The author could visualize even greater benefits if the committee commissioned a series of task forces comprising representatives of higher education (presidents of community colleges, liberal arts colleges, private urban universities, comprehensive state universities, land-grant colleges and universities; deans and faculty members of these institutions; trustees; deans and faculty members of extension divisions and evening colleges; and leaders of institutions prominent in the client systems of higher adult education) to develop guidelines for a given classification as indicated in the outline in Appendix A. Such a plan would have two big advantages over the committee-promulgated process: (1) it would itself be an educational process in which key leaders in the universities would become better informed about adult education and (2) the university community would have a deeper commitment to guidelines it had helped to create.

Perhaps the committee will have accomplished its goal, however, if by publishing this study it stimulates universities to launch their own processes for developing guidelines and assessing their policies and practices.

2 Higher Adult Education in Perspective

The only true perspective on higher adult education in the United States is kaleidoscopic, for its evolution has consisted of shifting patterns of variegated bits and pieces. As Lyman Bryson pointed out a generation ago, the general American adult education movement has not been of a single and systematic character (as in many other countries and in other areas of American education); it always has been carried on by a wide variety of agencies, for a variety of purposes, and with many different kinds of people. For this reason some critics have called it formless and without direction, though actually it has penetrated more phases of life in this than in any other country and has expressed the complexity and vitality of American life.[1] The same observations can certainly be made about higher adult education. And, although it is reassuring to think that higher adult education expresses the complexity and vitality of American life, this does not simplify the task of interpreting it to the policymakers, administrations, and faculties of universities or to the public.

A HISTORICAL SYNOPSIS

University professors had been experimenting with extension lectures, often in collaboration with libraries, long before any formal structure for higher adult education was established.[2] Shortly after the end of the Civil War more formalized programs using university personnel were developed by the lyceums and the Chautauqua Institution. But the idea of institutionalized university extension was brought to this country by returning scholars from England, where it had taken shape at Oxford and Cambridge in the 1870s. Extension divisions were established at the Universities of Wisconsin and Kansas in 1891, at the University of Chicago in 1892 (where extension was one of five fundamental divisions at the time of that institution's founding), and at a few other universities after the turn of the century. These early extension activities, modeled after the English lecture-examination format, tended to lose popularity after initial bursts of enthusiasm.

The turning point in American university extension came with the reorganization of the extension division at the University of Wisconsin in

1. *Adult Education* (New York: American Book Co., 1936), pp. 13–14.
2. For the most comprehensive historical overviews of higher adult education see: Carey, 1961; Dyer, 1956; Knowles, 1962; Liveright and Miller, 1960; and Morton, 1953.

1906–07 as a service agency with responsibility for helping to meet the needs of government, agriculture, industry, and the adult public so as to make the boundaries of the university campus coincide with the boundaries of the state. This new public service spirit quickly spread to other universities, and in 1915 the National University Extension Association was founded with a membership of twenty-two institutions that had more or less formally organized extension divisions.

From its earliest stages the program of university extension was highly heterogeneous and unintegrated. The first services established were lecture series, evening classes, correspondence courses, and conference activities. But gradually, in response to public pressures and imaginative leadership, other nonacademic activities, such as short-term institutes, short courses, traveling libraries, publication services, exhibits, advisory services, tours, and classes at distant points by circuit-riding instructors, were added.

Thus evolved one of the three main tributaries of the stream of higher adult education in this country. To distinguish it from the others, it has become known widely as General Extension.

A second tributary was the almost parallel development in the land-grant colleges across the country of what for a long time was called Agricultural Extension. As land-grant colleges were established following the Morrill Act of 1862, they engaged increasingly in extension teaching services with farmers' institutes, farmers' unions, farm bureaus, and other agricultural societies. As agricultural education grew in scope and complexity in these new colleges of agricultural and mechanical arts, pressure mounted for federal leadership of the movement. After several attempts at congressional legislation failed, the Smith-Lever Act establishing the Cooperative Extension Service was passed and signed by President Wilson in May 1914.

Under this law a national network was established in which the basic unit was a staff of workers employed by each county and serviced by a cooperative extension division in each land-grant college. A Federal Extension Service in the Department of Agriculture provided research, information, and training services. Originally concerned primarily with improving the farmer as a producer of feed and fiber, the cooperative extension continuously broadened its scope to encompass the welfare of farmers and their families and, most recently, the improvement of community life in suburban and even urban areas.

In the development of methods and materials uniquely tailored to the education of adults, agricultural extension's contributions have been outstanding. It pioneered techniques for producing and evaluating actual changes in practices. It perfected techniques of home visitation and result demonstration as the most effective instruments of change, although, as the educational level of the rural population rose, increasing use was made of group meetings and mass media. Without doubt it went farther than any other agency in developing procedures for systematically involving its constituency in the program-planning process through the use of a variety of committees and councils. It refined procedures for preparing and pretesting such materials as teaching aids; staff-training manuals; leaflets, digests, and reports of research; and publications keyed to the reading levels of particular audiences. Finally, it set the pace for adult education in the collection of reliable statistics; its annual reports, *Extension Activities and Accomplishments,* have been the most comprehensive statistical reports of adult educational participation in the entire field.

As the program and clientele of the cooperative extension service have become increasingly geared to the needs and conditions of an urban civilization, pressure has mounted for closer collaboration, if not merger, between the general and agricultural extension services of the state university systems.

The third main tributary of the higher adult education stream was the evening college movement that developed in the private, and particularly in the urban, universities beginning in the late nineteenth century. Originally established when young adults demanded that they be allowed to continue their baccalaureate studies part time while working full time, the early evening college programs consisted essentially of the same courses offered to day students. But as the pace of technological and social change has accelerated, evening colleges have developed special programs to help people meet the changing conditions of work, family life, leisure, and public affairs.

A part of the headwaters of higher adult education is the hundreds of independent liberal arts colleges and technological institutions that do not have organized extension divisions or evening colleges, but offer myriad educational services to their alumni and their surrounding communities. A study in 1953 showed that of 404 independent liberal arts colleges responding to a questionnaire, 233 had some adult educational activities serving almost 45,000 adults.[3]

Further enriching this picture of the historical evolution of higher adult education are the countless independent springs that have bubbled up in the universities from time to time. Schools of medicine, dentistry, education, business, social work, fine arts, engineering, theology, and others have instituted both short-term and long-term continuing educational programs for members of their professions. Radio and television stations have been established as autonomous operations. Audiovisual centers, library extension services, and urban affairs centers have gone into the community with public services. Many individual professors have contracted independently

3. Crimi, 1957.

with community institutions for consultation, training, lecturing, and other services.[4]

Finally, while adult education has been expanding into a more central position in the university system, these same trends have been occurring in public school systems, libraries, business and industry, governmental agencies, voluntary organizations, and religious institutions. The problem of delineating the appropriate unique roles, constituencies, and services of these suppliers of adult education is just being recognized. Some attempts have been made to create mechanisms for coordination or joint planning, such as community, state, and national adult educational councils or associations, but their success has been limited.[5]

THE CURRENT PICTURE

Although the kaleidoscope of higher adult education hardly stays still long enough for a current snapshot to be taken, and the data-collection processes are still too primitive to yield a complete and accurate picture, the following seem to be the highlights of the current situation as revealed in the existing literature: [6]

Adult education is carried on in a wide variety of institutions of higher education:

> Some states have comprehensive state-wide systems (Oregon).
>
> All states have land-grant universities.
>
> Some states have, in addition, separate state universities (University of Michigan at Ann Arbor).
>
> Some states have comprehensive state universities (University of Wisconsin).
>
> Some states have sectional state institutions (state colleges at Boston, Framingham, Fitchburg, Salem, etc., in Massachusetts).
>
> Many states have secular private universities (Harvard, Northeastern, Boston University).
>
> Many states contain religious private universities (Saint Louis University).
>
> Many states have public and private specialized institutions (technical institutes, theological seminaries, teachers colleges).
>
> Many states have private liberal arts colleges (Antioch in Yellow Springs, Ohio; Goddard in Plainfield, Vermont).
>
> Some states have private junior colleges offering adult educational services, and most states have a growing number of public community colleges.

4. Burch, 1961.
5. Knowles, 1962.
6. The most comprehensive statistical sources are: Crimi, 1957; Johnstone and Rivera, 1965; Joint AUEC-NUEA Committee, 1964 and 1966; Morton, 1953; and Thornton, 1966.

No mechanism exists for coordination of the adult educational activities of all these institutions at any level. But informal exchanges of information take place in some communities (adult education councils) and regions (regional boards or associations), and in some states (Oregon, New York) mechanisms exist for coordination of activities in public institutions. At the national level, exchange of information takes place through the National Association of State Universities and Land-Grant Colleges, the Association of University Evening Colleges, the National University Extension Association, and the Adult Education Association of the U.S.A.

The number of registrations in higher adult education activities in the mid-1960s was estimated variously at from 2,500,000 to 4,354,000, reflecting both the problem of definitions and the inadequacy of data-collection machinery in the field.[7] But estimators agreed that the growth rate during the 1960s was better than 10 percent.[8]

A wide variety of activities is employed for the education of adults in institutions of higher education, including: [9]

> Regular university courses originally developed for young people but scheduled at times or places convenient for adults.
>
> Lengthy course sequences designed especially for adults. Specially designed courses, lecture series, or discussion groups.
>
> Special activities (concerts, exhibitions, or lectures) provided on the campus for the members of the academic community and local residents.
>
> Correspondence study programs.
>
> Short course and conference programs.
>
> Radio and television programs.
>
> Provision of instructional materials to groups or individuals.
>
> Programs designed to aid local communities in analyzing and solving their problems.
>
> Programs to aid special occupational groups.
>
> The cooperative extension program.
>
> Services provided for other public or private institutions. Educational programs designed particularly for the university's alumni.
>
> Specialized program services for clubs and associations. Speakers' bureaus.
>
> Production or publication of educational materials.
>
> Organized services for foreign students and visitors to the campus.
>
> Sponsorship of leagues or competitions in music, art, drama, speech, etc.

7. Johnstone and Rivera, 1965; Joint AUEC-NUEA Committee, 1964; Frandson, 1967; Liveright, 1968, p. 63.

8. Frandson, 1967; Joint AUEC-NUEA Committee, 1964.

9. Houle and Nelson, 1956; *University Extension Makes a Difference in Wisconsin* (Madison: University of Wisconsin, 1967).

Articulated Instructional Media (AIM) programs.

Multimedia community educational projects.

Consultative or reference bureaus.

Organized tours.

The organizational and administrative arrangements that exist for the management of services to adults vary so widely as to defy clear classification. A few generalizations will illustrate this condition: [10]

All land-grant and comprehensive state universities have extension divisions. In most of these universities, cooperative extension, located administratively in the School of Agriculture, operates apart from general extension, which may be responsible directly to the president or to a vice-president or dean of faculties. In a growing number of universities, cooperative and general extension are unified under a single administrator with their operations coordinated in varying degrees.

Most private and public urban universities have evening colleges, colleges of general studies, or divisions of continuing education. Some of these merely manage the scheduling, registration, and operating processes for activities planned and controlled by academic departments and professional schools; others have full autonomy in operating their own programs with their own faculties and in some cases giving their own degrees.

In a small proportion of the other types of institutions (sectional state institutions, liberal arts colleges, specialized institutions, and community colleges) services to adults are coordinated by a separate administrative unit; in most of them such services are an optional responsibility of a public relations office, an alumni office, an assistant to the president, or the individual academic departments.

Two explanations for this state of affairs are noteworthy:

Carey's "growth cycle" theory holds that adult divisions go through typical stages of growth which can be charted:

The first stage is that of *departmental domination.* In this stage the control of the faculty, programs, and resources is located in the regular departments and the adult division may have only part-time leadership.

The second stage reveals the impulse toward *autonomous development.* The adult enterprise enters this stage only when it escapes departmental domination.

The third stage occurs after a period of autonomous operation. It is the stage of *movement toward integration.* The independence of the evening college or extension division is no longer threatened by close ties with the campus.

10. These generalizations are drawn from: Carey, 1961; Crimi, 1957; Daigneault, 1959 and 1963; DeCrow, 1962; Dyer, 1956; Gould, 1961; Houle, 1959; Houle and Nelson, 1956; Liveright and Miller, 1960; McMahon, 1960b; Morton, 1953; Petersen, 1960; and Shannon and Schoenfeld, 1965.

Rather, there is a recognition of the need for campus resources in doing a more effective job.

Finally, there is the stage of *assimilation*. In this stage the adult education function is recognized as a legitimate university concern and the adult division is accepted as a peer in the university family. Now the adult division has a well-developed notion of its service area and it is free to move within the university system to meet the needs of its many publics.[11]

Houle and Nelson explain that

As a university develops its services for adults, there usually comes a time when they grow too large to be regarded any longer as a miscellaneous assemblage of particular activities scattered throughout the institution. At this point, two basic policies come into conflict. The first grows out of the need to consider adult education as an extension of the whole university, with the careful preservation of the right of the respective departments and schools to establish and maintain standards which their subject-matter or professional responsibilities dictate. The second policy springs from the need to coordinate the work in the field so that there can be proper focus and balance of services in terms of the needs and interests of the mature clientele, and so that the resources of the institution will be used carefully and economically. Every university must somehow work out a balance between these two general policies.

No two universities have worked out the same balance, and none of them is satisfied with the pattern that it now has. The literature on university adult education is filled with analyses of the problem of how the university may best organize itself to discharge its adult educational function, but so far the questions raised vastly exceed the answers that have been found.[12]

A problem of organization, perhaps unique to the adult educational segment of the general educational enterprise, is the role of the clientele in program development and operation. It is a cardinal principle in adult education that provision be made in the organizational structure for participants' representation in the decision-making process. Many public school evening programs, for example, have citizen's advisory councils; most voluntary agency programs have program-planning committees; and cooperative extension uses county advisory committees. There is strong evidence from studies of these programs that their strength and quality correlate directly with the strength and quality of client representation in planning. But the tradition is strong in higher education that decisions about program are made by the faculty; there are few examples across the country of mechanisms created to involve community representatives in planning courses for the adult constituencies of the universities.

The policies and practices concerning the faculty of higher adult education vary almost as widely as the organizational arrangements:

Five different faculty systems are used in staffing evening college and university extension programs in varying combinations among the universities:[13]

11. Carey, 1961, p. 11.
12. Houle and Nelson, 1956, pp. 75-76.
13. Burch, 1961, pp. 38-39; Carey, 1961, pp. 106-107.

1. Appointment of full-time separate faculty to the extension operation—a practice employed widely only in cooperative extension.

2. Assignment of "campus" faculty to teaching in extension as part of their regular duties.

3. Employment of regular faculty in extension on an overload basis for which additional compensation is given.

4. Employment of part-time nonfaculty, whose qualifications are reviewed and approved by appropriate university departments.

5. Employment for informal classes of outside teachers whose only qualifications are demonstrated mastery of a given subject and capacity to teach it to adults and who are not subject to faculty review.

Evening colleges tend to hold to a fifty-fifty balance between teachers from campus and community, while extension divisions lean toward a higher percentage from the campus.[14]

Overload payments to regular faculty practically never approach what they are paid for an equal amount of teaching as part of their regular faculty load.[15]

Seven different payment plans for part-time faculty are employed, often in combination within a single university:[16]

1. Specified amount for each course taught.

2. Specified salary for the term.

3. Specified annual salary.

4. An amount dependent upon income from course.

5. Specified amount for each class taught.

6. Payments varying with each course, ranging from $7.50 for a class session to $50.

7. Specified amount for each clock hour, depending upon rank.

There is little evidence that the part-time teacher is encouraged to utilize his professional competence in curriculum planning or other professional activities, that he is taken into the faculty as a professional equal, or that he is treated by the university administration as a valuable professional asset.[17]

Only a small proportion of the administrators and faculties of higher adult education have had any professional training specifically in the theory and practice of educating adults, and few universities have more than a superficial orientation for their faculties to the unique requirements of adult education.[18]

14. Carey, 1961, p. 106.
15. DeCrow, 1962, p. 31.
16. Morton, 1953, p. 84.
17. Gowin and Daigneault, 1961, p. 7.
18. Carey, 1961; DeCrow, 1962; Dyer, 1956; Gowin and Daigneault, 1961.

Extension teaching is usually rated low in the reward system on which status and professional advancement are based in the university.[19]

The policies and practices of financing higher adult education are varied, but the following broad generalizations are made in the literature: [20]

The absence of standard budgetary procedures precludes an accurate estimate of the total expenditures for higher adult education, but it is estimated that in 1962 the 72 NUEA institutions alone earmarked over $50 million for general extension and in 1964 the land-grant colleges and universities budgeted nearly $178 million for cooperative extension.[21]

Usually, general extension services are required to pay their own way or make a profit, leading to a "market economy" in which a premium is placed on courses that are certain to have a large enrollment. This policy tends to restrict risk capital for new program development and to eliminate programs and clientele of great social significance.

General extension, because of state support, is somewhat less dependent on student tuition than are evening colleges.

There is little reliable information on the amount of state subsidy for extension activities from state to state or on policies concerning financial support.

Cooperative extension, funded jointly by federal, state, and county governments, has a tradition of free service. General extension must often charge relatively large fees. Public expectations of the university are therefore confused, and the coordination of these two services is difficult.

There is practically no endowment support for any part of higher adult education.

University faculty members provide a massive subsidy to extension programs by teaching at overload rates drastically lower than their regular salaries.

Budget and accounting procedures are lacking in uniformity and clarity, creating many problems: coordination and control are difficult; budget officers tend to become policymakers; cost projections become troublesome.

Cooperative extension has greatly augmented its resources by using volunteer leaders and teachers; general extension has no such tradition.

Increased federal support for particular services (Poverty Program

19. Carey, 1961; DeCrow, 1962; Dyer, 1956; Petersen, 1960.
20. See Carey, 1961; English, 1965; Kidd, 1962; Morton, 1953; Petersen, 1960.
21. Shannon and Schoenfeld, 1965.

training, Peace Corps training, basic education training, etc.) is relieving some financial pressures but is exerting influences for program development in directions not necessarily congruent with client needs or university goals.

A substantial volume of higher adult educational services are provided outside the academic institutions:

Business and industrial corporations provide in-plant programs affecting millions of employees and their families in many subject fields, including general education, technical and scientific disciplines, management and supervision, human relations, and cultural appreciation.[22]

Governmental agencies, especially the military services, the Civil Service Commission, and the Graduate School of the Department of Agriculture, operate a vast program of education for adults in many of the same areas covered by university extension.[23]

Many professional associations, such as the American Management Association, the American Hospital Association, and the American Nurses Association, and many voluntary organizations, such as the National Council of the YMCA and the American National Red Cross, carry on extensive programs of personnel development which encompass areas of study similar to those in university extension.[24]

A vast array of proprietary schools, including correspondence schools, technological institutes, business colleges, etc., provide adult educational services in a variety exceeding those of all universities combined.[25]

An estimated nine million adults, many of them at the level of higher adult education, are engaged in systematic independent study with and without the aid of library readers' services, commercial instructional guides, commercial programmed instruction, and other help.[26]

22. Burton Clark, 1964; Clark and Sloan, 1962; Serbein, 1961.
23. Clark and Sloan, 1964; Houle, 1947; Knowles, 1960, pp. 238–54; Knowles, 1962, pp. 98–103.
24. Johnstone and Rivera, 1965; Knowles, 1960 and 1962.
25. Knowles, 1960 and 1962.
26. Johnstone and Rivera, 1965.

3 Forces for Change
in Higher Adult Education

Many forces outside the universities are promoting an academic revolution.

There are technological changes bringing increasingly heavy demands for talent. The knowledge explosion makes an engineer, a pharmacist, or a physician out of date almost before the ink is dry on his diploma. A demand is rising for upgraded skills for old jobs and new skills for new jobs.

There is the realization that wasted talent inhabits both slums and suburbia, that many people, if given a chance, could move along the educational track to productive roles in society. Prison reform fairly shouts for rehabilitative educational programs. The handicapped call for education. The talents of many women lie idle. The aged could be more productive—and happier. Cultural deprivation faces not just those in the ghettoes but also those in the suburbs. People are deprived of educational opportunities as much by geographical handicaps as by finances.

There is an awareness that we are a poorly informed citizenry, that many of us do not understand the world in which we live, to say nothing of the international, national, and local issues we should be resolving as voting citizens.

There is concern about using our leisure time; increasing productivity of both farm and factory; meeting problems of the community; resolving social ills of race, poverty, health, land use, pollution, and a thousand others. Concern is increasing over the adjustment from a rural to an urban society and the resulting change in values.

Broadly conceived, these are the *outside* forces pushing universities along the road of revolution—an academic revolution still in its incipient stage, but one so great that eventually it will transform the role of the modern American university in society.

More specifically, the following forces are assaulting the ivory towered citadels directly:

First, the impact of the federal government. Just as research gradually has been built into most federal legislation since the late 1940s, now exten-

This chapter is adapted from a memorandum by Donald R. McNeil, chancellor, University Extension, University of Wisconsin. See also: Adolfson, 1961; Blackwell, 1961 and 1967; Burns, 1964; Carey, 1961; Cummings, 1967; Daigneault, 1959; DeCrow, 1964; Haygood, 1962; Ingham, 1966; Klotsche, 1966; Leagans, 1966; Liveright, 1968; Matre, 1962; Mead, 1961; Michigan State University, 1968; Miller, 1966; National Agricultural Extension Center, 1962; NUEA, 1961; Shannon, 1965; Taylor, 1961; Theobold, 1964.

sion is being built in. There has been a role for higher adult education in almost every piece of recent social legislation. The Elementary and Secondary Education Act, the Higher Education Act, the Manpower Development and Training Act, the Vocational Education Act, the Public Health Service Act, the Housing and Urban Development Act, and the Foreign Assistance Act all have extension built in.[1]

Moreover, the Office of Economic Opportunity has put tremendous demands upon universities for training—of Vista volunteers, job corpsmen, community action leaders, Headstart teachers, and rural leaders. The military services want an accelerated higher continuing education program; the Department of Labor seeks help in retraining officials, as does the Department of Housing and Urban Development. The Office of Civil Defense has contracts for training programs with a number of universities. And the Department of Health, Education, and Welfare has, of course, become a gigantic client of the universities.

Houle observes that federal policies affecting higher adult education seem to be changing, postulating that the following shifts may be occurring: [2]

From a policy that adult education be used only to advance the economic resources of the country, to a policy that it be used to achieve many different purposes.

From a policy that federal funds be used to extend the coverage of prototype institutions and services, to a policy that they be used to create new educational forms and activities.

From a policy that the federal government has no responsibility for the coordination of its adult educational efforts, to an increasingly widespread belief that it has some responsibility to coordinate these efforts.

From a policy that the federal government should place its major emphasis in adult education outside the Office of Education, leaving it concerned chiefly with childhood education in formal schools and colleges, to a policy that the Office of Education should both sponsor its own adult education programs and help coordinate federal activities.

From a policy that, in its grant-in-aid programs of adult education, the federal government should work with and through a few institutions serving as chosen administrative instruments, to a policy that, in such programs, the government should work with and through many institutions.

From a policy that, in its grant-in-aid programs, the federal government should establish broad policy and fiscal control but allow

1. *Federal Support for Adult Education* (Washington, D.C.: Adult Education Association, 1968).

2. Cyril O. Houle, "Federal Policies Concerning Adult Education," *School Review* 76 (June 1968): 166–89.

great freedom to the states and institutions with which it works, to a policy (changing, amidst many denials) that the government should exercise continuing control over the programs that it initiates or establishes.

The state and local governments, too, are increasing their demands on universities. Paralleling federal demands, states are asking universities to train officials—administrators, social workers, conservation wardens, prison officials, sanitary engineers, county board members, public health workers, councilmen, policemen, and practically the whole range of civil servants. More than training, though, many states conceive of the university's extension role in the broader context of applying research to the solving of social ills. Universities become planning and policy resources as well as educational mechanisms when they work with state agencies in highway safety, pollution control, conservation practices, land-use management, regional planning, welfare programming, the elimination of illiteracy and poverty, health practices, and economic development. At the local level, universities are asked to work in all these fields plus those peculiar to a particular locality.

Occupational groups, too, are pressing universities. Professional groups—lawyers, physicians, engineers—are particularly demanding. By the nature of their positions in the volatile educational world, teachers consistently demand continuing education. Business, industry, and labor are turning to universities more and more as they realize that training is an increasingly specialized undertaking. Community organizations are calling on universities to give their professional and volunteer workers the continuing in-service training they need.

INSIDE FORCES

Significant forces *inside* the universities promote the academic revolution as well. More presidents are making honest commitments to extension and supporting their actions with hard dollars and real talent. New structures are evolving. In land-grant institutions, reorganization and merger are the themes. In November 1966, seventeen administrators of merged or coordinated (cooperative and general extension) divisions met in Washington; by the beginning of 1969, twenty-two universities had either merged divisions or established a general university office to coordinate extension and public service activities.

There are glimpses of a changing reward system that gives more compensation and status to a professor for involvement in extension teaching. Subsidy to extension programs is increasing in both public and private institutions. Adequate space is becoming available. A genuine interest in continuing education is growing among administrators, faculty members, department chairmen, and deans. We detect a new realization that there must be an interplay between campus and society, that involvement with the educational needs beyond the campus will directly affect research and teaching on the campus.

Observers of the contemporary social scene seem to agree that strong forces are at work both outside and inside the American institutions of higher education creating pressures toward an "adult education explosion."

to its community. For example, it may operate a film library, provide consultants and technical services to municipalities, sponsor concerts and other cultural events, and the like.[13]

4. Extending its present program to the community is at best an inadequate conception of higher education's responsibilities for the education of adults. The weakness of much higher adult education lies in the mimicry of traditional curricula—the lack of imagination that creates new approaches to the education of adults. The university should actively study the educational needs of communities and individual adults. In these needs it will find not only new areas where education should be provided but also the seeds of new subject matter and research problems. All the activities that bring the university into vital interaction with society should be viewed together, whether or not they fit the traditional labels of extension or adult education. Similarly, the implications of lifelong learning for the present undergraduate and graduate programs should be examined.[14]

Although generalizations in such a complex field are always questionable, the literature gives the impression that the first position is widely held by evening and junior college adult education administrators. Some version of the second and third positions represents the thinking of most general extension administrators, would be common in public junior and community colleges with active community programs, and would be approved by many university evening college deans. The fourth position is seriously advocated by relatively few university adult educators, although recent position papers by the National University Extension Association and the General Extension Division of the National Association of State Universities and Land-Grant Colleges suggest that general extension administrators may be moving (or, some would say, returning) to this broader view. With little modification, the fourth position represents the spirit of cooperative extension throughout its history and is increasingly propounded in the literature of the community college movement.

THE CLIENTELE

Except for the annual reports of the Cooperative Extension Service, the statistics of higher adult education are at best incomplete and at worst confusing. Partial enrollment surveys (partial in that not all types of institutions were included) were made by Morton in 1951–52; the Joint Committee on Minimum Data and Definitions of the Association of University Evening Colleges and NUEA in 1960–61, 1962–63, and 1965–66; Johnstone in 1962–63; Thornton (community colleges) in 1964; and Frandson in 1967. Hard evidence is available, therefore, only for short-

13. Burch, 1961; Daigneault, 1959; Petersen, 1960.
14. Blackwell, 1967; Burch, 1961; Cummings, 1967; Franklin, 1966; Hamilton, 1964; Horn, 1964; Liveright, 1966; Petersen, 1960; Tolley, 1967; Willie, 1967.

4 Trends in Higher Adult Education Today

How is higher adult education responding to the forces for change? There has been a crescendo of interest in the recent literature of higher adult education in identifying contemporary trends.[1] Much agreement appears among the observers concerning general directions of movement, but supporting evidence is often lacking or inconclusive. The difference between "what is" and "what ought to be" is not always clear.

CONCEPT AND CLIMATE OF ADULT EDUCATION

The concept of "lifelong learning" is taking on a new meaning. Until recently it meant accumulating during youth much of the knowledge one needed for the rest of his life, then making up deficiencies as they appeared during the adult years. In this concept adult education had a strong remedial flavor because of the twin assumptions that education is a transmission process for existing knowledge and a function primarily of youth.

But, as Whitehead pointed out a generation ago, we are living in the first period of human history for which these assumptions are false:

The note of recurrence dominates the wisdom of the past, and still persists in many forms even where explicitly the fallacy of its modern application is admitted. The point is that in the past the time-span of important change was considerably longer than that of a single human life. Thus mankind was trained to adapt itself to fixed conditions. But today this time-span is considerably shorter than that of a human life, and accordingly our training must prepare individuals to face a novelty of conditions.[2]

If it is true that the time span of major cultural change is now less than the lifetime of a human being, the needs of society and of individuals can no longer be served by education that merely transmits knowledge and is concentrated in the years of youth. *The new world requires a new purpose for education—the development of a capacity in each individual to learn, to change, to create a new culture throughout his life span.* The central mission of elementary, secondary, and collegiate education must become, then, not

1. See especially: Blackwell, 1967; Boone, 1962; Briley, 1966; Burch, 1961; Carey, 1961; Cummings, 1967; Daigneault, 1959; Haygood, 1962; Houle, 1959 and 1967; Klotsche, 1966; Knowles, 1962; Kravitz, 1967; Leagans, 1966; Liveright, 1959; Liveright and Miller, 1960; Liveright and Goldman, 1965; Liveright, 1960 and 1968a; McNeil, 1967; Michigan State University, 1968; Miller, 1966; Shannon and Schoenfeld, 1965; Tolley, 1967.
2. Alfred N. Whitehead. Introduction to *Business Adrift,* by Wallace B. Donham (New York: McGraw-Hill Book Company, 1931), pp. viii–xix.

teaching youth what they need to know but teaching them how to learn what is not yet known. The substance of youth education, therefore, becomes process; the process of learning and the substance of adult education becomes content—the content of man's continually expanding knowledge.

There is evidence that this new concept of lifelong learning has already greatly influenced the frontier workers in elementary and secondary education; the "new curricula" in mathematics, science, and social studies are organized around the notion of teaching youngsters to inquire rather than just to absorb knowledge. There is less evidence of change in collegiate education, although some of the experimentation with group and individual independent study takes this direction. But major energy currently is devoted in higher adult education to developing new curriculum theories, special degree programs, and educational counseling services that provide a sequential continuity of learning experiences throughout the adult years.[3]

Flowing from this broadened concept is the wider acceptance of continuing education as a necessary component in a total educational design and not merely as an afterthought when the needs of the young have been served. As national concern increases and legislation is enacted to finance continuing education, adult education is accepted as an essential ingredient in the national educational approach to social betterment.[4]

Agencies of the federal government, through legislation and financial support, as well as private foundations and individual educational institutions are gradually enlarging the scope of their commitment to continuing education to include liberal as well as vocational education and urban as well as agricultural and rural education.[5]

Whenever federal funds for community and continuing education are allocated, there is likely to be a provision calling for state and local community initiative and planning concerning local programs. Such provisions encourage cooperative efforts between public and private agencies on behalf of continuing education activities.[6]

Business corporations and other agencies representing society's nongovernmental sector are also enlarging their commitment to continuing education, expanding their own internal programs, and contributing more regularly and fully to community programs. In addition, businesses (e.g., publishers) that produce materials for adult education are increasing their investment and output.[7]

3. Blackwell, 1961; Farmer, 1967; Jensen, 1964; Knowles, 1962; Liveright and DeCrow, 1963; Liveright and Goldman, 1965; Mead, 1961; Taylor, 1961; Thompson, 1967; Whipple, 1957.
4. DeCrow, 1964; Liveright and Goldman, 1965; Liveright, 1968.
5. Haygood, 1962; Houle, 1959; Liveright and Goldman, 1965; Liveright, 1968.
6. Haygood, 1962; Liveright and Goldman, 1965; Liveright, 1968.
7. Liveright and Goldman, 1965.

Continuing education is developing international significance. Because of the acute need for adult education in the developing nations, institutions of higher education in the United States are increasing their contributions to international projects and organizations; in a few cases, they are actually establishing outposts of their extension programs in overseas areas.[8]

It has been pointed out repeatedly that the United States today is in a position of leadership in a world-wide movement for continuing education, sharing that position with Great Britain but to some extent dominating. Our actions matter abroad and, reciprocally, what adult educators do in other countries influences us. The danger is that university adult educators tend to be so preoccupied with maintaining their own operations that they have little energy left to perform their leadership roles.[9]

THE UNIVERSITY'S ROLE

Among those who agree that the university has a definite responsibility for the education of adults (and in our review of the literature written by or addressed to university adult educators, we found no opposition to this view), opinion varies widely on what, precisely, are the most appropriate and useful functions of the evening college or extension service. These views may be summarized in four positions along a continuum from least to greatest involvement in the education of adults:[10]

1. In general, the university should do what it uniquely is able to do well, i.e., provide high quality degree and credit courses. Adult students are, on the whole, similar in their educational needs and motivations to regular students. They want college-grade education and degrees of unquestioned quality. The task is to make the regular university program easily available to adults.[11]

2. In addition to degree and credit courses, the university should provide noncredit short courses, conferences, and other informal educational opportunities for adults. It should be alert to correspondence study, educational radio and television, or other means of extending its resources. All these programs should, of course, be meaningful educational experiences, organized for significant learning of complex subject matter requiring participation of the university faculty.[12]

3. The university may appropriately provide, in addition to its educational programs, a variety of services that might not otherwise be available

8. Liveright and Goldman, 1965; Liveright, 1968.
9. Adolfson, 1961; Bebout, 1963; Blackwell, 1967; Cummings, 1967; DeCrow, 1964; Haygood, 1962; Horn, 1967; Houle and Nelson, 1956; Klotsche, 1966; Knowles, 1963; Liveright, 1968; McGrath, 1963; McNeil, 1967; Southern Regional Education Board, 1963; Taylor, 1961.
10. References simply provide illustrations of statements concerning a position and do not necessarily indicate that the author subscribes to that position.
11. Houle, 1954; Matre, 1965; McGheen, 1954; McNeil, 1963.
12. Hamilton, 1964; Horn, 1964; Houle, 1954; Kidd, 1962.

term trends; long-run trends are largely based on estimates and conference reports. Even with hard data, however, the nature of higher adult education presents inherent problems for statistical comparisons. For instance, how are units of participation in a three-day workshop compared with units in a 45-hour semester-length course? Within these limitations, the following trends in clientele are identified in the literature:

Participation has been rapidly increasing in higher adult education. Morton estimated a 70 percent growth in enrollment between 1930 and 1940—from 150,000 to 220,000—in "organized and continuing instructional programs" in the 76 NUEA member institutions.[15] By 1951–52 the enrollment had increased to 1.5 million, a growth of 600 percent in 10 years.[16]

Both Johnstone and the Joint AUEC-NUEA Committee on Minimum Data and Definitions estimated enrollments of around 2.5 million in 1961–62, but since their estimates were based on different definitions from Morton's, comparisons would be misleading (note that Johnstone's estimates are limited to participation in two forms of adult education, courses and independent study.[17] The joint AUEC-NUEA committee reported a total of 4,354,000 registrations for classes, correspondence education, institutes, workshops, and discussion groups in 245 AUEC and NUEA institutions in Canada and the United States in 1964–65.[18]

Projections indicate that the student body of higher adult education will continue to grow. Applying the present growth rates in adult education participation, Johnstone estimates a 50 percent increase in the general field in the 20-year interval, 1962–82. He notes, however, that college-level adult education will increase at a greater rate:

The most important conclusion to be derived from this study is that America is likely to experience an adult education explosion during the next few decades . . . Even very conservative projections suggest that within two decades the population will contain as many as 64 per cent more adults who have been to college, 59 per cent more who have attended high school, and by contrast, some 15 per cent fewer with only a grade-school education. . . . It should be abundantly clear, then, that the potential audience for adult education is increasing at a much faster rate than the population as a whole. Just as in the fifties and sixties the regular school system had to tool up rapidly to accommodate the greatly increased numbers of young persons in the population, so too in the seventies and eighties adult education will be subject to greatly increased demands as this group moves into the social categories where greatest uses are made of adult education.[19]

15. Morton, 1953, p. 46.
16. *Ibid.,* p. 134.
17. Johnstone and Rivera, 1965, p. 61; Joint AUEC-NUEA Committee, 1964, p. 5. See also Frandson, 1967, pp. 7–9.
18. Joint AUEC-NUEA Committee, 1964.
19. Johnstone and Rivera, 1965, pp. 19–20.

The joint AUEC-NUEA committee, on the other hand, projects a 300 percent increase in registrations from 2.5 million in 1961–62 to 11,760,000 in 1980.[20]

The participants in higher education are increasingly well-educated. As Houle points out:

There are several good reasons why the rise in campus enrolments will be paralleled by a rise in adult enrolments. The most fundamental cause is that, as a college education and advanced degrees become more widely accepted as essential for the young, they will be desired by an increasing number of adults . . . The formally educated person is the one who participates in adult educational activities; as one level of education increases, so will the other.[21]

Since it is estimated that the number of college graduates will more than double between 1960 and 1980, the presumption is that an increasing proportion of participants in continuing education will be college graduates.[22] These graduates will be better educated in another sense too: they will have been taught in their formal schooling to take more responsibility for inquiry than was the case with the present adult generation.

The clientele of higher adult education is being increasingly defined to include organizations and communities as well as individuals. Although statistical data do not yet exist to support this trend, the periodical literature with increasing frequency describes university services to "client systems" such as government agencies, corporations, voluntary organizations, and community development authorities. A substantial body of literature in recent years deals with the theory and practice of the university's role as an agent of institutional change, with special reference to ways universities can improve the educative quality of the environments of all human institutions.[23]

CURRICULUM, TEACHING, AND SERVICES

Clearly the field of higher adult education—and, for that matter, the entire field of adult education—is in a state of ferment over curriculum theory and instructional technology. American adult education theorists are dipping heavily into theoretical works by European adult educators, especially German and Yugoslavian, which have accumulated since the late nineteenth century under the label *andragogy*. Derived from the stem of the Greek word for mature male, *Aner* (*Andros*), this label distinguishes the study of adult learning and teaching from the study of youth learning and teaching symbolized by the label *pedagogy*. There is developing, ac-

20. Joint AUEC-NUEA Committee, 1964, p. 5.
21. Houle, 1959, p. 6.
22. *Statistical Abstract of the U.S.*, 1961, p. 108.
23. Haygood, 1962; Knowles, 1962, pp. 278–79; Kravitz, 1967.

cordingly, a coherent and comprehensive theory of adult learning and a differentiated technology of adult education.[24]

At this time andragogical theory is largely speculative, but it is being increasingly subjected to empirical research. The four main sets of assumptions on which current andragogical theory is based have to do with differences between children and youth as to (1) self-concept, (2) experience, (3) readiness to learn, and (4) orientation to learning.

Under the first assumption, as a person matures his self-concept moves from that of a dependent personality toward that of a self-directed organism. Accordingly, mature people learn best in educational situations where the students and teacher have a relationship of mutual responsibility for diagnosing learning needs, formulating objectives, and planning, conducting, and evaluating learning experiences.

Secondly, since the mature person has accumulated a substantial reservoir of experience, he has a broader foundation on which to build, and he is himself a richer resource for learning than when he was younger. The adult, therefore, learns best through methods and techniques that use his experience. Hence there is a marked shift in adult education away from the transmittal techniques of lecture and assigned reading toward the action-learning techniques of community projects, case method, critical incident process, discussion, simulation exercises, and the like.

Thirdly, the mature person confronts a set of developmental tasks different from those of youth; youth's developmental tasks concern preparing and becoming, i.e., self-identity, whereas the adult's developmental tasks concern performance in the changing roles of worker, spouse, parent, and responsible citizen. At any point in time an adult is prepared to learn what is required by his developmental tasks at that time; accordingly, a mature person learns best in a curriculum sequenced to coincide with his developmental tasks.

In the fourth place, the mature person approaches learning with a time perspective different from that of youth. The adult intends to apply immediately what he learns, whereas the youth intends to postpone application of most of his learning. As a result, the youth approaches learning in a subject-centered frame of mind, while the adult brings a problem-

24. For elaboration on studies of adult learning and andragogical theory, see: Edmund deS. Brunner et al., *An Overview of Adult Education Research* (Washington, D.C.: Adult Education Association, 1959), pp. 8–162; J. Roby Kidd, *How Adults Learn* (New York: Association Press, 1959); Malcolm S. Knowles, ed., *Handbook of Adult Education in the U.S.* (Washington, D.C.: Adult Education Association, 1960), pp. 54–95; Malcolm S. Knowles, "Andragogy, Not Pedagogy!" *Adult Leadership* 16 (April 1968): 350–86; Raymond G. Kuhlen, ed., *Psychological Backgrounds of Adult Education* (Syracuse, N.Y.: Center for the Study of Liberal Education for Adults, 1963); Harry L. Miller, *Teaching and Learning in Adult Education* (New York: Macmillan Co., 1964), pp. 1–236; and Dusan Savicevic, "Training Adult Educationists in Yugoslavia," *Convergence* 1 (March 1968): 69–75.

centered frame of mind. Accordingly, the mature person learns best through activities organized around immediate life problems, rather than around logical subject development.

As these concepts are increasingly translated into practice, the curriculum and teaching methodology of extension looks less and less like the curriculum and methodology of the programs designed for youthful day students.

The following trends are discernible in this contemporary ferment of adult program development:

There is a tendency toward greater flexibility in the manner in which adults can work toward a baccalaureate degree. Mainly this flexibility is accomplished by allowing credit through proficiency examination; by developing special degree programs for adults that combine regular courses, independent study, short-term residential seminars, correspondence study, and mass media programs; and by relaxing the traditional residence requirements. Various degree programs developed especially for adults are now in operation at Boston University, Brooklyn College, Queens College, the University of Oklahoma, Syracuse University, Goddard College, Johns Hopkins University, and New York University and are under consideration by faculty committees at the University of Hawaii, the State University of New York at Buffalo, the University of South Florida, and several others.[25]

The new formats for adult learning invented in recent years are rapidly exceeding traditional credit courses in student participation. These formats include training institutes, residential laboratories, informal courses, community development projects, multimedia package programs, organizational change projects, telecourses, workshops, educational tours, and a variety of informal educational services.[26]

The special problems of urban living and of the increasing urbanization of society in general are causing urban universities to become more deeply involved in research and educational programs directly concerned with city living and city planning. Several universities have created special administrative units (e.g., urban affairs centers) to conduct research, offer instruction, or provide services related to urban problems. Others have incorporated these activities into the existing pattern of operation. Especially noticeable is the expansion of programs in manpower development and community leadership for ghetto residents. Some states, notably Wisconsin, have established urban extension agents who serve urban areas in the same way that agricultural extension agents have served rural

25. College Entrance Examination Board, 1967; Flaugher, 1967; Liveright and DeCrow, 1963; Liveright and Goldman, 1965; Whipple, 1957.

26. Franklin, 1966; Glancy, 1958; Haygood, 1962; Liveright and Goldman, 1965; White, 1964; University of California, 1963; University of Iowa, 1967.

4 Trends in Higher Adult Education Today

How is higher adult education responding to the forces for change? There has been a crescendo of interest in the recent literature of higher adult education in identifying contemporary trends.[1] Much agreement appears among the observers concerning general directions of movement, but supporting evidence is often lacking or inconclusive. The difference between "what is" and "what ought to be" is not always clear.

CONCEPT AND CLIMATE OF ADULT EDUCATION

The concept of "lifelong learning" is taking on a new meaning. Until recently it meant accumulating during youth much of the knowledge one needed for the rest of his life, then making up deficiencies as they appeared during the adult years. In this concept adult education had a strong remedial flavor because of the twin assumptions that education is a transmission process for existing knowledge and a function primarily of youth.

But, as Whitehead pointed out a generation ago, we are living in the first period of human history for which these assumptions are false:

> The note of recurrence dominates the wisdom of the past, and still persists in many forms even where explicitly the fallacy of its modern application is admitted. The point is that in the past the time-span of important change was considerably longer than that of a single human life. Thus mankind was trained to adapt itself to fixed conditions. But today this time-span is considerably shorter than that of a human life, and accordingly our training must prepare individuals to face a novelty of conditions.[2]

If it is true that the time span of major cultural change is now less than the lifetime of a human being, the needs of society and of individuals can no longer be served by education that merely transmits knowledge and is concentrated in the years of youth. *The new world requires a new purpose for education—the development of a capacity in each individual to learn, to change, to create a new culture throughout his life span.* The central mission of elementary, secondary, and collegiate education must become, then, not

---

1. See especially: Blackwell, 1967; Boone, 1962; Briley, 1966; Burch, 1961; Carey, 1961; Cummings, 1967; Daigneault, 1959; Haygood, 1962; Houle, 1959 and 1967; Klotsche, 1966; Knowles, 1962; Kravitz, 1967; Leagans, 1966; Liveright, 1959; Liveright and Miller, 1960; Liveright and Goldman, 1965; Liveright, 1960 and 1968a; McNeil, 1967; Michigan State University, 1968; Miller, 1966; Shannon and Schoenfeld, 1965; Tolley, 1967.
2. Alfred N. Whitehead. Introduction to *Business Adrift*, by Wallace B. Donham (New York: McGraw-Hill Book Company, 1931), pp. viii–xix.

teaching youth what they need to know but teaching them how to learn what is not yet known. The substance of youth education, therefore, becomes process; the process of learning and the substance of adult education becomes content—the content of man's continually expanding knowledge.

There is evidence that this new concept of lifelong learning has already greatly influenced the frontier workers in elementary and secondary education; the "new curricula" in mathematics, science, and social studies are organized around the notion of teaching youngsters to inquire rather than just to absorb knowledge. There is less evidence of change in collegiate education, although some of the experimentation with group and individual independent study takes this direction. But major energy currently is devoted in higher adult education to developing new curriculum theories, special degree programs, and educational counseling services that provide a sequential continuity of learning experiences throughout the adult years.[3]

Flowing from this broadened concept is the wider acceptance of continuing education as a necessary component in a total educational design and not merely as an afterthought when the needs of the young have been served. As national concern increases and legislation is enacted to finance continuing education, adult education is accepted as an essential ingredient in the national educational approach to social betterment.[4]

Agencies of the federal government, through legislation and financial support, as well as private foundations and individual educational institutions are gradually enlarging the scope of their commitment to continuing education to include liberal as well as vocational education and urban as well as agricultural and rural education.[5]

Whenever federal funds for community and continuing education are allocated, there is likely to be a provision calling for state and local community initiative and planning concerning local programs. Such provisions encourage cooperative efforts between public and private agencies on behalf of continuing education activities.[6]

Business corporations and other agencies representing society's non-governmental sector are also enlarging their commitment to continuing education, expanding their own internal programs, and contributing more regularly and fully to community programs. In addition, businesses (e.g., publishers) that produce materials for adult education are increasing their investment and output.[7]

3. Blackwell, 1961; Farmer, 1967; Jensen, 1964; Knowles, 1962; Liveright and DeCrow, 1963; Liveright and Goldman, 1965; Mead, 1961; Taylor, 1961; Thompson, 1967; Whipple, 1957.
4. DeCrow, 1964; Liveright and Goldman, 1965; Liveright, 1968.
5. Haygood, 1962; Houle, 1959; Liveright and Goldman, 1965; Liveright, 1968.
6. Haygood, 1962; Liveright and Goldman, 1965; Liveright, 1968.
7. Liveright and Goldman, 1965.

Continuing education is developing international significance. Because of the acute need for adult education in the developing nations, institutions of higher education in the United States are increasing their contributions to international projects and organizations; in a few cases, they are actually establishing outposts of their extension programs in overseas areas.[8]

It has been pointed out repeatedly that the United States today is in a position of leadership in a world-wide movement for continuing education, sharing that position with Great Britain but to some extent dominating. Our actions matter abroad and, reciprocally, what adult educators do in other countries influences us. The danger is that university adult educators tend to be so preoccupied with maintaining their own operations that they have little energy left to perform their leadership roles.[9]

THE UNIVERSITY'S ROLE

Among those who agree that the university has a definite responsibility for the education of adults (and in our review of the literature written by or addressed to university adult educators, we found no opposition to this view), opinion varies widely on what, precisely, are the most appropriate and useful functions of the evening college or extension service. The views may be summarized in four positions along a continuum from least to greatest involvement in the education of adults:[10]

1. In general, the university should do what it uniquely is able to do well, i.e., provide high quality degree and credit courses. Adult students are, on the whole, similar in their educational needs and motivations to regular students. They want college-grade education and degrees of unquestioned quality. The task is to make the regular university program easily available to adults.[11]

2. In addition to degree and credit courses, the university should provide noncredit short courses, conferences, and other informal educational opportunities for adults. It should be alert to correspondence study, educational radio and television, or other means of extending its resources. All these programs should, of course, be meaningful educational experiences, organized for significant learning of complex subject matter requiring participation of the university faculty.[12]

3. The university may appropriately provide, in addition to its educational programs, a variety of services that might not otherwise be available

8. Liveright and Goldman, 1965; Liveright, 1968.

9. Adolfson, 1961; Bebout, 1963; Blackwell, 1967; Cummings, 1967; DeCrow, 1964; Haygood, 1962; Horn, 1967; Houle and Nelson, 1956; Klotsche, 1966; Knox, 1963; Liveright, 1968; McGrath, 1963; McNeil, 1967; Southern Regional Education Board, 1963; Taylor, 1961.

10. References simply provide illustrations of statements concerning each position and do not necessarily indicate that the author subscribes to that position.

11. Houle, 1954; Matre, 1965; McGheen, 1954; McNeil, 1963.

12. Hamilton, 1964; Horn, 1964; Houle, 1954; Kidd, 1962.

to its community. For example, it may operate a film library, provide consultants and technical services to municipalities, sponsor concerts and other cultural events, and the like.[13]

4. Extending its present program to the community is at best an inadequate conception of higher education's responsibilities for the education of adults. The weakness of much higher adult education lies in the mimicry of traditional curricula—the lack of imagination that creates new approaches to the education of adults. The university should actively study the educational needs of communities and individual adults. In these needs it will find not only new areas where education should be provided but also the seeds of new subject matter and research problems. All the activities that bring the university into vital interaction with society should be viewed together, whether or not they fit the traditional labels of extension or adult education. Similarly, the implications of lifelong learning for the present undergraduate and graduate programs should be examined.[14]

Although generalizations in such a complex field are always questionable, the literature gives the impression that the first position is widely held by evening and junior college adult education administrators. Some version of the second and third positions represents the thinking of most general extension administrators, would be common in public junior and community colleges with active community programs, and would be approved by many university evening college deans. The fourth position is seriously advocated by relatively few university adult educators, although recent position papers by the National University Extension Association and the General Extension Division of the National Association of State Universities and Land-Grant Colleges suggest that general extension administrators may be moving (or, some would say, returning) to this broader view. With little modification, the fourth position represents the spirit of cooperative extension throughout its history and is increasingly propounded in the literature of the community college movement.

THE CLIENTELE

Except for the annual reports of the Cooperative Extension Service, the statistics of higher adult education are at best incomplete and at worst confusing. Partial enrollment surveys (partial in that not all types of institutions were included) were made by Morton in 1951–52; the Joint Committee on Minimum Data and Definitions of the Association of University Evening Colleges and NUEA in 1960–61, 1962–63, and 1965–66; Johnstone in 1962–63; Thornton (community colleges) in 1964; and Frandson in 1967. Hard evidence is available, therefore, only for short-

13. Burch, 1961; Daigneault, 1959; Petersen, 1960.
14. Blackwell, 1967; Burch, 1961; Cummings, 1967; Franklin, 1966; Hamilton, 1964; Horn, 1964; Liveright, 1966; Petersen, 1960; Tolley, 1967; Willie, 1967.

term trends; long-run trends are largely based on estimates and conference reports. Even with hard data, however, the nature of higher adult education presents inherent problems for statistical comparisons. For instance, how are units of participation in a three-day workshop compared with units in a 45-hour semester-length course? Within these limitations, the following trends in clientele are identified in the literature:

Participation has been rapidly increasing in higher adult education. Morton estimated a 70 percent growth in enrollment between 1930 and 1940—from 150,000 to 220,000—in "organized and continuing instructional programs" in the 76 NUEA member institutions.[15] By 1951–52 the enrollment had increased to 1.5 million, a growth of 600 percent in 10 years.[16]

Both Johnstone and the Joint AUEC-NUEA Committee on Minimum Data and Definitions estimated enrollments of around 2.5 million in 1961–62, but since their estimates were based on different definitions from Morton's, comparisons would be misleading (note that Johnstone's estimates are limited to participation in two forms of adult education, courses and independent study.[17] The joint AUEC-NUEA committee reported a total of 4,354,000 registrations for classes, correspondence education, institutes, workshops, and discussion groups in 245 AUEC and NUEA institutions in Canada and the United States in 1964–65.[18]

Projections indicate that the student body of higher adult education will continue to grow. Applying the present growth rates in adult education participation, Johnstone estimates a 50 percent increase in the general field in the 20-year interval, 1962–82. He notes, however, that college-level adult education will increase at a greater rate:

The most important conclusion to be derived from this study is that America is likely to experience an adult education explosion during the next few decades . . . Even very conservative projections suggest that within two decades the population will contain as many as 64 per cent more adults who have been to college, 59 per cent more who have attended high school, and by contrast, some 15 per cent fewer with only a grade-school education. . . . It should be abundantly clear, then, that the potential audience for adult education is increasing at a much faster rate than the population as a whole. Just as in the fifties and sixties the regular school system had to tool up rapidly to accommodate the greatly increased numbers of young persons in the population, so too in the seventies and eighties adult education will be subject to greatly increased demands as this group moves into the social categories where greatest uses are made of adult education.[19]

15. Morton, 1953, p. 46.
16. *Ibid.,* p. 134.
17. Johnstone and Rivera, 1965, p. 61; Joint AUEC-NUEA Committee, 1964, p. 5. See also Frandson, 1967, pp. 7–9.
18. Joint AUEC-NUEA Committee, 1964.
19. Johnstone and Rivera, 1965, pp. 19–20.

The joint AUEC-NUEA committee, on the other hand, projects a 300 percent increase in registrations from 2.5 million in 1961–62 to 11,760,000 in 1980.[20]

The participants in higher education are increasingly well-educated. As Houle points out:

> There are several good reasons why the rise in campus enrolments will be paralleled by a rise in adult enrolments. The most fundamental cause is that, as a college education and advanced degrees become more widely accepted as essential for the young, they will be desired by an increasing number of adults . . . The formally educated person is the one who participates in adult educational activities; as one level of education increases, so will the other.[21]

Since it is estimated that the number of college graduates will more than double between 1960 and 1980, the presumption is that an increasing proportion of participants in continuing education will be college graduates.[22] These graduates will be better educated in another sense too: they will have been taught in their formal schooling to take more responsibility for inquiry than was the case with the present adult generation.

The clientele of higher adult education is being increasingly defined to include organizations and communities as well as individuals. Although statistical data do not yet exist to support this trend, the periodical literature with increasing frequency describes university services to "client systems" such as government agencies, corporations, voluntary organizations, and community development authorities. A substantial body of literature in recent years deals with the theory and practice of the university's role as an agent of institutional change, with special reference to ways universities can improve the educative quality of the environments of all human institutions.[23]

CURRICULUM, TEACHING, AND SERVICES

Clearly the field of higher adult education—and, for that matter, the entire field of adult education—is in a state of ferment over curriculum theory and instructional technology. American adult education theorists are dipping heavily into theoretical works by European adult educators, especially German and Yugoslavian, which have accumulated since the late nineteenth century under the label *andragogy*. Derived from the stem of the Greek word for mature male, *Aner (Andros)*, this label distinguishes the study of adult learning and teaching from the study of youth learning and teaching symbolized by the label *pedagogy*. There is developing, ac-

20. Joint AUEC-NUEA Committee, 1964, p. 5.
21. Houle, 1959, p. 6.
22. *Statistical Abstract of the U.S.*, 1961, p. 108.
23. Haygood, 1962; Knowles, 1962, pp. 278–79; Kravitz, 1967.

cordingly, a coherent and comprehensive theory of adult learning and a differentiated technology of adult education.[24]

At this time andragogical theory is largely speculative, but it is being increasingly subjected to empirical research. The four main sets of assumptions on which current andragogical theory is based have to do with differences between children and youth as to (1) self-concept, (2) experience, (3) readiness to learn, and (4) orientation to learning.

Under the first assumption, as a person matures his self-concept moves from that of a dependent personality toward that of a self-directed organism. Accordingly, mature people learn best in educational situations where the students and teacher have a relationship of mutual responsibility for diagnosing learning needs, formulating objectives, and planning, conducting, and evaluating learning experiences.

Secondly, since the mature person has accumulated a substantial reservoir of experience, he has a broader foundation on which to build, and he is himself a richer resource for learning than when he was younger. The adult, therefore, learns best through methods and techniques that use his experience. Hence there is a marked shift in adult education away from the transmittal techniques of lecture and assigned reading toward the action-learning techniques of community projects, case method, critical incident process, discussion, simulation exercises, and the like.

Thirdly, the mature person confronts a set of developmental tasks different from those of youth; youth's developmental tasks concern preparing and becoming, i.e., self-identity, whereas the adult's developmental tasks concern performance in the changing roles of worker, spouse, parent, and responsible citizen. At any point in time an adult is prepared to learn what is required by his developmental tasks at that time; accordingly, a mature person learns best in a curriculum sequenced to coincide with his developmental tasks.

In the fourth place, the mature person approaches learning with a time perspective different from that of youth. The adult intends to apply immediately what he learns, whereas the youth intends to postpone application of most of his learning. As a result, the youth approaches learning in a subject-centered frame of mind, while the adult brings a problem-

24. For elaboration on studies of adult learning and andragogical theory, see: Edmund deS. Brunner et al., *An Overview of Adult Education Research* (Washington, D.C.: Adult Education Association, 1959), pp. 8–162; J. Roby Kidd, *How Adults Learn* (New York: Association Press, 1959); Malcolm S. Knowles, ed., *Handbook of Adult Education in the U.S.* (Washington, D.C.: Adult Education Association, 1960), pp. 54–95; Malcolm S. Knowles, "Andragogy, Not Pedagogy!" *Adult Leadership* 16 (April 1968): 350–86; Raymond G. Kuhlen, ed., *Psychological Backgrounds of Adult Education* (Syracuse, N.Y.: Center for the Study of Liberal Education for Adults, 1963); Harry L. Miller, *Teaching and Learning in Adult Education* (New York: Macmillan Co., 1964), pp. 1–236; and Dusan Savicevic, "Training Adult Educationists in Yugoslavia," *Convergence* 1 (March 1968): 69–75.

centered frame of mind. Accordingly, the mature person learns best through activities organized around immediate life problems, rather than around logical subject development.

As these concepts are increasingly translated into practice, the curriculum and teaching methodology of extension looks less and less like the curriculum and methodology of the programs designed for youthful day students.

The following trends are discernible in this contemporary ferment of adult program development:

There is a tendency toward greater flexibility in the manner in which adults can work toward a baccalaureate degree. Mainly this flexibility is accomplished by allowing credit through proficiency examination; by developing special degree programs for adults that combine regular courses, independent study, short-term residential seminars, correspondence study, and mass media programs; and by relaxing the traditional residence requirements. Various degree programs developed especially for adults are now in operation at Boston University, Brooklyn College, Queens College, the University of Oklahoma, Syracuse University, Goddard College, Johns Hopkins University, and New York University and are under consideration by faculty committees at the University of Hawaii, the State University of New York at Buffalo, the University of South Florida, and several others.[25]

The new formats for adult learning invented in recent years are rapidly exceeding traditional credit courses in student participation. These formats include training institutes, residential laboratories, informal courses, community development projects, multimedia package programs, organizational change projects, telecourses, workshops, educational tours, and a variety of informal educational services.[26]

The special problems of urban living and of the increasing urbanization of society in general are causing urban universities to become more deeply involved in research and educational programs directly concerned with city living and city planning. Several universities have created special administrative units (e.g., urban affairs centers) to conduct research, offer instruction, or provide services related to urban problems. Others have incorporated these activities into the existing pattern of operation. Especially noticeable is the expansion of programs in manpower development and community leadership for ghetto residents. Some states, notably Wisconsin, have established urban extension agents who serve urban areas in the same way that agricultural extension agents have served rural

25. College Entrance Examination Board, 1967; Flaugher, 1967; Liveright and DeCrow, 1963; Liveright and Goldman, 1965; Whipple, 1957.
26. Franklin, 1966; Glancy, 1958; Haygood, 1962; Liveright and Goldman, 1965; White, 1964; University of California, 1963; University of Iowa, 1967.

areas for over half a century, and bills have been introduced repeatedly in Congress for a national urban extension program.[27]

Special programs to meet the unique needs of women as a separate audience are being developed across the country. Pioneered at the University of Minnesota, Radcliffe College, Simmons College, and Northeastern University, these programs have spread to other universities in one form or another.[28]

The average citizen's increased interest in the arts and in cultural activities generally has pressed universities into a more active role in providing for the cultural needs of their communities. This trend is notable among the smaller liberal arts colleges.[29]

Attention to adult educational counseling, as an integral part of continuing education and especially as an aid to independent study, is increasing. Specially trained adult counselors are working particularly with programs for women and with special-degree programs for adults, but they also appear increasingly on extension division and evening college staffs. The adult educational counselor performs a unique function in higher adult education by providing the sequential planning and "course articulation" which in degree programs for undergraduates are provided inherently in the curriculum organization.[30]

Increased attention is given to in-service training for adult education faculty in the concepts and skills of the new adult educational technology. A few universities (notably Rutgers, Drake, Northeastern, Oklahoma, and Syracuse) have developed elaborate programs of in-service education, but the literature abounds with criticisms that most adults are still taught with traditional curricula and methods.[31]

Concepts of academic excellence and standards of evaluation are developing which are geared to the unique functions of higher adult education and the unique characteristics of adults as learners. But traditional definitions of academic standards are deeply rooted, and most higher adult education is still evaluated on the same scales (grade point averages, content covered, etc.) as youth education, whether they are relevant or not. Some observers find this the single greatest block to the development of stronger general university extension programs. This has never been a factor in

27. Bailey, 1967; Blackwell, 1967; Gordon, 1967; Haygood, 1962; Klotsche, 1966; Kravitz, 1967; Liveright and Goldman, 1965; Willie, 1967.

28. Goldman, 1961; Liveright and Goldman, 1965.

29. Goldman, 1961 and 1966; Liveright and Goldman, 1965.

30. Farmer, 1967; Liveright and Goldman, 1965; Thompson, 1967; Winters, 1961.

31. Burkett and Ruggiers, 1965; DeCrow, 1962; Dyer, 1956; Glancy, 1958; Gowin, 1961; Horn, 1964; Houle, 1960; Liveright and Goldman, 1965; McGhee, 1954; McMahon, 1960b.

cooperative extension, where the principal evaluative measure has been behavioral change.[32]

The plea for different concepts of academic excellence and standards of evaluation is made not because extension students are less able than their undergraduate counterparts but because they are more mature. Studies show that in both scholastic aptitude and academic achievement the distribution of extension students has a median which is at or, more usually, above that of regular students and the dispersion is greater at both ends.[33]

Implications of the concept of continuing education for the education of undergraduates are beginning to receive attention. The idea of lifelong learning implies basic changes in existing undergraduate programs to build in a desire for postschool learning early in the student's academic career, instill the motivation for continuing education, and provide the skills of self-directed inquiry. In fact, there is some evidence that undergraduates learn better when taught according to andragogical principles, for by late adolescence an individual has acquired most of the adult characteristics.[34]

Some analysts of higher education are attributing the current unrest on college campuses to the pedagogical orientation of undergraduate curricula, teaching, and governance. Kenneth D. Roose, vice-president of the American Council on Education, sees a promising line of development here as the effort "to meet student demands for reform of undergradaute education by incorporating much of the teaching methods and programmatic experiences of continuing education." [35]

Starting from the premise that learning is a lifelong process, assumptions about the education of undergraduates may be drawn from the literature of adult education:

1. The purpose of education for the young must shift from transmission of knowledge—its current primary focus—to development of the learning capacity.

2. The curriculum of education for the young must shift from a subject-mastery basis to a learning-skill basis of organization.

3. The teacher's role must be redefined from "one who primarily transmits knowledge" to "one who primarily helps students to inquire."

4. New criteria must be applied to determine readiness to leave full-time schooling: (*a*) Has the student mastered the tools of learning?

32. Bye, 1958; Cundiff, 1958; Horn, 1964; Liveright and Goldman, 1965; NUEA, 1962.

33. DeCrow, 1959.

34. For reports of studies supporting this generalization, see the following pamphlets in the U.S. Office of Education series, *New Dimensions in Higher Education:* No. 1, "Independent Study"; No. 5, "Management of Learning"; No. 7, "Quest for Quality"; and No. 10, "Flexibility in the Undergraduate Curriculum" (Washington, D.C.: Government Printing Office, 1960–62).

35. Kenneth D. Roose to Malcolm S. Knowles, 5 November 1968.

(*b*) Has he developed an insatiable appetite for learning? (*c*) Does he have a definite, but flexible, plan for continuing his learning?

The author of these assumptions goes on to suggest that:

It would help to symbolize the concept of learning as a lifelong process if every institution for the education of youth would convert its graduation ritual into an exchange between the student, who would hand the president a scroll detailing his plans for continuing learning, and the head of the institution, who would hand the student a certificate stating that the institution has taught the student all it now knows about how to learn but will continue to make its resources available to him for further inquiry.[36]

Attention to developing educational programs and services for alumni and other members of the college and university community is increasing. Lifelong learning implies that undergraduate activities should be buttressed by educational counseling that continues after graduation, by expanded educational opportunities for alumni, and by opportunities for participation in continuing and integrated educational programs for all the adults of the community.[37]

An effort to develop total university programs based on the concept of continuity has begun. At Oakland University in Michigan, for example, extension personnel have analyzed the concept in an extended seminar with the regular faculty; preparatory (for continuing education) seminars for undergraduates have been introduced; continuing counseling has been established for graduates; and the alumni program emphasizes educational activities. In connection with its program for women, the University of Minnesota has experimented with a special seminar to help undergraduate women look to and beyond the child-rearing years to future needs and opportunities for continuing education. And the University of Pittsburgh has announced a community-wide approach to continuing education.[38]

ORGANIZATION AND ADMINISTRATION

The development of higher adult education as an organizational system can be viewed from two perspectives: (1) structures for coordination among universities at the national, regional, state, and metropolitan levels and (2) structures for operation within an individual institution.

Structures for Coordination Among Universities

The general coordinative agencies of higher education (American Association of Junior Colleges, American Council on Education, Association for Higher Education, the National Association of State Universities and Land-Grant Colleges) *have increased attention to adult education in their conference programs, committee structures, and publications.* But they are only beginning to formulate policies concerning the role of higher

36. Knowles, 1962, pp. 273–76.
37. Liveright, 1966.
38. Liveright and Goldman, 1965, pp. 22–23; Knowles, 1962, pp. 273–76.

education in adult education and the role of adult education in institutions of higher education.[39]

The specialized national agencies for higher adult education (AUEC and NUEA) *have cooperated closely with each other and especially with their former joint service agency, the Center for the Study of Liberal Education for Adults, in legislative activities.* Both organizations are working to bring a sense of coherence, unity, direction, status, professionalism, and integrity to the field of higher adult education.[40]

Regional educational boards and associations are taking a larger part in providing for higher continuing education, in planning and promoting regional activities, and in providing for the professional development of adult educators. Supported by an advisory council of educators and legislators, the Southern Regional Education Board is conducting an energetic program of professional development and regional planning for continuing education. In the Northeast, a council on continuing education is being established through the efforts of the New England Board of Higher Education, which sponsored a national conference on adult counseling in 1965 with CSLEA.[41]

Some states are moving toward coordination and central planning in continuing higher education. In several states, studies have been undertaken recently on the adequacy of continuing education as a part of the total appraisal of educational needs and resources. The California Coordinating Council for Higher Education issued a prototype "Status Report on Continuing Education Programs in California Higher Education" in 1965. In Ohio, a 1966 study leading to a master plan for the Board of Regents included a survey of the present program and future needs in higher adult education. In a northern Indiana regional study of opportunities for higher education, the CSLEA was asked to investigate the need for liberal education for adults. Oregon has had a state-wide unified system of higher education for some time, and movements along similar lines are under way in Nebraska, New York, and Utah. The Massachusetts Advisory Council on Education is preparing a plan for state-wide coordination to be announced in 1969. In fact, developments such as these in many states are so rapid that up-to-date information about them is not available from any central source.[42]

39. Adolfson and others, 1961; Drazek, 1965; Grinager, 1964; Houle, 1959; Miller, 1966; Thornton, 1966; Tyler, 1961.

40. AUEC, 1965; Carey, 1961; Daigneault, 1959; DeCrow, 1964; Joint AUEC-NUEA Committees, 1964 and 1966; Liveright, 1960; Lockwood, 1960; NUEA, 1961.

41. Liveright and Goldman, 1965, pp. 13–14; Southern Regional Education Board, 1963.

42. Liveright and Goldman, 1965; Ohio Board of Regents, 1966; State University of New York, 1965 and 1967. See also *Status Report on Continuing Education Programs in California Higher Education* (Sacramento: California Coordinating Council for Higher Education, November 1965).

In a few metropolitan areas such as Chicago, Denver, New York, and Boston, mechanisms for information exchange and joint planning have been instituted, sometimes through a local adult educational council, but more often through informal relationships. On the whole, higher adult education is still an open market with competition more apparent than coordination.[43]

Structures for Higher Adult Education Within an Institution

There seems to be a tendency toward consolidation and centralization of responsibility for the planning and operation of continuing education within individual institutions, but there are enough opposing examples to require serious qualifications about this generalization. In some institutions, such as the University of Denver and the University of Chicago, credit courses formerly managed by extension divisions have been turned over to the campus departments and schools. But in others, such as the University of California, Boston University, and The American University, all credit and noncredit courses, special degree programs, and conferences and institutes designed specifically for adult students have been assigned to the continuing education unit. A number of attempts, notably at Michigan State University, have been made to devise mechanisms for bringing academic departments and continuing education divisions into a partnership in the operation of continuing education programs. Perhaps the safest generalization about the current trend in organization is that universities across the country are reassessing their institutional arrangements and experimenting with a wide variety of administrative patterns.[44]

Reexamination of the relationship between general and cooperative extension in the land-grant universities is leading to a consolidation of the two divisions in many institutions. Among the first states to effect such a consolidation were Missouri, West Virginia, Nebraska, Utah, and Wisconsin. In addition, specific plans to study or move toward a combined extension service are projected in Alabama, California, Connecticut, Maine, Minnesota, Oklahoma, Oregon, and Virginia.[45]

THE PERSONNEL

The personnel of higher adult education fall into several categories: (1) full-time administrative workers; (2) faculty who teach full time in continuing education (including cooperative extension agents); (3) faculty whose main load is campus courses but who teach part time in

43. Knowles, 1962, pp. 176–83.
44. Briley, 1966; Burch, 1961; Carey, 1961; Daigneault, 1963; DeCrow, 1962; Dyer, 1956; Houle, 1959; Liveright and Goldman, 1965; McMahon, 1960; Pennsylvania State University, 1960; Petersen, 1960; Shannon and Schoenfeld, 1965; State University of New York, 1965 and 1967; Stern, 1961.
45. Houle, 1959; Liveright and Goldman, 1965; McNeil, 1963; Petersen, 1960; Shannon and Schoenfeld, 1965.

continuing education; (4) citizens recruited from outside the university to teach part time; and (5) professors of adult education who train professional adult educational workers. Comprehensive statistics have never been compiled, but these populations number well over 50,000 and are growing rapidly.

The following trends are observed in the literature:

Administrative roles in higher adult education, traditionally seen largely as stepping stones to higher positions, are increasingly perceived as career specializations. Historically, administrators of extension divisions or evening colleges were faculty members or administrators from other posts within the university, assigned for an indefinite period to the continuing education operation. Few had any special training in adult education. But in recent years more "adult-educators-by-accident" have engaged in summer workshops or degree programs in adult education with a view to remaining as career specialists in this field. It is noteworthy, too, that university administrators are looking increasingly for trained adult educators to fill openings as they occur in continuing education administration. No doubt this increased professionalization has been facilitated by a steady rise in salary and by the marked advance in status of the extension director in the university (such as to chancellor at Wisconsin; vice-chancellor at Oregon; executive dean at the State University of New York; and vice-president at California, Michigan State, Missouri, and Syracuse).[46]

Although the number of faculty assigned to teach full time in continuing education is gradually increasing, the rate of increase is not as great as that of part-time teachers. Full-time adult education teachers are found predominantly in university colleges and special-degree programs in general extension and among state specialists and county staffs in cooperative extension. Among inhibiting factors in developing full-time faculties are the part-time nature of most adult education and the fact that the adult division typically carries less prestige than the day departments.[47]

There is a growing discontent with the reward system among faculty who teach part time in continuing education. Compensation for teaching evening courses is almost universally lower than that for regular campus courses, and, typically, little credit toward promotion is gained from participation in extension work. This situation makes it difficult to recruit the best teachers for extension and to persuade them to give the time required for in-service education.[48]

There is a growing discontent also with the limitations placed on

46. AUEC, 1965; Carey, 1961; DeCrow, 1962; Morton, 1953; Schroeder, 1965; Tolley, 1967.
47. DeCrow, 1962; McMahon, 1960; Stern, 1961.
48. DeCrow, 1962; Dyer, 1956; McNeil, 1967; Petersen, 1960.

extension administrators in recruiting and retaining talent from outside the university. Traditional criteria for faculty selection and promotion—degrees, research, publications, teaching experience—do not necessarily reflect the qualities required for excellence in teaching adults. Furthermore, the social system, organized exclusively around undergraduate and graduate education, tends not to provide for the part-time continuing education teacher either a definable status or the opportunity to participate in decisions affecting his welfare. The contemporary literature is replete with demands for the revision of university faculty policies so as to take into account the differential function of extension teaching.[49]

Universities providing graduate training in adult education are increasing, but not as rapidly as the demand for professional workers. Some 25 universities now offer doctorates in adult education in the United States and Canada, and perhaps as many others provide some work at the master's level. But every professor of adult education receives requests for trained workers which total many times the size of his graduating class each year.[50]

FINANCIAL POLICIES AND PRACTICES

The variation in budgetary practices among colleges and universities and the total absence of any central data bank on extension finances make it impossible to get evidence of specific trends as to money spent for what purposes by whom. But trends of a general nature are clearly discernible in the contemporary literature:

Discontent is growing among administrators of higher adult education over financial policies and practices imposed on them by general university tradition and policy. The most frequently cited causes of discontent are: (1) There is a double standard in financial policy: except in the Cooperative Extension Service, adults pay their own way, whereas youth are subsidized. This policy puts the general extension divisions under pressure to skew their programs to money-making activities (large credit classes and popular noncredit activities) and limits experimental funds. The result is a tendency to use the courses of the day departments unchanged. (2) When state aid is given, it often is loaded with the pet projects of pressure groups and too often is ephemeral; it is the first item to be reduced when a new administration enters office. (3) Fiscal policies and practices of the central administrations, and especially attitudes of budget officers, tend to be geared to the operation of stable programs for full-time students. But, as Carey found:

49. Burch, 1961; Bye, 1958; Carey, 1961; Carlin, 1964; Cundiff, 1958; Daigneault, 1963; DeCrow, 1962; Dyer, 1956; Gould, 1961; Gowin, 1961; Horn, 1964; Houle, 1959; Liveright, 1966; Matre, 1965; McMahon, 1960; McNeil, 1963; Petersen, 1960.
50. Jensen, 1964.

The adult division characteristically offers a wide diversity of courses, both credit and noncredit. Demands from the community for short courses and institutes or for special programs are quite likely to be sporadic. The undergraduate and graduate divisions are in a much better position to estimate their yearly budgetary requirements since most of their students are registered for a sequential credit program leading to a degree. Thus, while a rigid budget policy may be feasible and even desirable for the day divisions, this same policy can have serious effects on the adult operation. In some schools, the difficulty of transferring funds from one account to another during the year can result in the cancellation of courses.[51]

Recently when a distinguished gray-haired professional man applied for an installment tuition-payment plan at a university and was given a form to be signed by his parents or guardians, he was so embarrassed that he cancelled his enrollment. (4) Compensation policies, as pointed out previously, tend to discriminate against part-time faculties of the extension division.[52]

Concern is growing over the rising federal financing of higher adult education. As detailed in chapter 3, the volume of funds, diversity of purposes, complexity of conditions, and dispersion of funding agencies have increased enormously in recent years. This development has led to expressions of the following concerns in the literature: (1) With most federal funds designated for special projects rather than for support of basic continuing programs, the results are program fragmentation and diversion from central goals. (2) Since many federal projects are of a crash nature with short lead time for planning and unrealistic deadlines, they produce a diversion of energy from long-run objectives and a constant climate of crisis. (3) Status within and among institutions is strongly influenced by a dean's success in obtaining federal grants or contracts, producing a new spirit of competitiveness among colleagues and a tendency to value "grantsmanship" over broader professional competencies. (4) The large amount of paper work necessary to obtain and administer federal projects diverts time and energy from more important work. (5) Too often, federal grants for the output of services are made without adequate provision for the cost of training personnel or evaluating results. Consequently, many programs are improvised and shoddy.[53]

Although funds for aid to full-time young students in universities are increasing, scholarships usually are denied to part-time adult students. Yet the financial sacrifices required for adults to continue their education often are greater than for youth. A few universities have eliminated this dual policy, and some funds have become available to adult students for

51. Carey, 1961, p. 90.
52. Carey, 1961; Daigneault, 1959; DeCrow, 1962; Kidd, 1962; Liveright, 1960; Petersen, 1960; University of California, 1965.
53. DeCrow, 1964; Kidd, 1962; Liveright and Goldman, 1965; McNeil, 1963; University of California, 1965.

specialized purposes from government agencies such as the Office of Economic Opportunity, the Department of Labor, and the Office of Education. But adult students remain for the most part ineligible for financial aid.[54]

Special concern is expressed over the low level of fellowship support for graduate education of professional adult educators. The 40 to 50 universities currently offering graduate programs in adult education in the United States and Canada are producing only a fraction of the trained workers for whom institutions are begging each year. Yet many highly qualified and experienced applicants for admission to these programs are unable to enter graduate study because of their financial burdens.[55]

THE FACILITIES

Now that it has been recognized that adults learn better under conditions different from those typically provided for youth education, certain changes have been taking place in the physical facilities for adult education.

More universities are remodelling old or building new campus structures to provide a more adult environment for extension activities. As Harold J. Alford points out:

If quality of program is the chief goal, special facilities and trained staff are essential. Even if adults *were* just tall children, the use of desks and other equipment designed for the education of the young would be inappropriate for the education of adults. The fact is, however, that adults are not just tall children. In addition to desks and other equipment that fit them physically, it is appropriate for adults to expect surroundings which acknowledge their adulthood. Adults in the United States today seldom—except under duress, as in the army, prison, or a hospital ward—live in dormitory situations, with more than two or three in a room and group toilet and bath facilities down the hall. Adults—other than those in certain religious orders—do not seek out hard pallets in bare cells for sleeping and contemplative study. Adults in the United States today do not seek out uncomfortable seats, thin walls, poor food, or dull meetings.[56]

Accordingly, some of the most luxurious accommodations for living and conferring known in the history of inn-keeping can be found today on campuses across the country. They feature motel-quality living quarters, seminar rooms with oval tables and upholstered chairs, built-in audiovisual equipment, closed circuit television, coffee and ice service, lounges, bars, libraries, reading rooms, recreation facilities, modern art exhibits, thermostatically controlled heat and air conditioning, and ample parking.

The number of residential centers, a development pioneered by the University of Minnesota and Michigan State University and spurred by

54. Adult Education Association, 1966; Deters, 1963; English, 1965; Farmer, 1967; Gould, 1961; Kidd, 1962; Knowles, 1962, pp. 138–55; McNeil, 1963 and 1965; Ohio State University, 1967; Wientge, 1965.

55. Houle, 1959; Jensen, 1964; Liveright, 1968.

56. *Continuing Education in Action: Residential Centers for Lifelong Learning* (New York: John Wiley & Sons, 1968), pp. 44–45.

Kellogg Foundation grants, has been increasing rapidly. Alford lists 79 centers owned by or affiliated with universities and colleges in 1968.[57] Noteworthy in this development has been the conscious effort during planning to bring together the most creative architects and adult educators to devise ways of translating principles of adult learning into brick and mortar. The "maximum interaction" and "flexible subgrouping" concepts featured in the Center for Continuing Education at the University of Oklahoma exemplify this effort.

General extension, tending to follow the example of cooperative extension, takes an increasing proportion of its services to the people. The suburban campuses of New York University and Northeastern University and the extension centers of the Universities of Michigan, Wisconsin, Colorado, and Missouri are recent examples of this trend.[58]

GENERAL TRENDS AFFECTING CONTINUING HIGHER EDUCATION

The literature of adult education reveals certain trends in society and in the general field of adult education which bear on higher adult education.

Liveright identifies the following *demographic* trends:

1. The population explosion will continue.
2. There will be more younger and older people.
3. People will move more frequently.
4. People will continue to move to metropolitan areas.
5. Babies born in the first wave of the postwar boom have reached their twenties, making that population group about 35 million.
6. Women in the labor force will increase by nearly half a million a year.

He adds the following *technological and scientific* trends:

1. Knowledge and research findings will continue to expand exponentially.
2. Information storage and retrieval techniques will make possible the storage and recall of rapidly expanding knowledge as required.
3. Systems planning and operational research will increase efficiency greatly and broaden management sophistication.

Plus these *occupational and vocational* trends:

1. Fewer workers will be required for unskilled, manufacturing, and agricultural jobs.
2. More persons will be required for service and professional work.
3. More jobs for subprofessionals are probable.
4. More frequent shifts in jobs may be expected.

57. *Ibid.*, pp. 129–33.
58. Adult Education Association, 1953; Carey, 1961; Daigneault, 1959; Ford Foundation, 1966; Kellogg Foundation, 1960; Knowles, 1962; Liveright, 1966; Pitkin, 1956; University of Chicago, 1965.

5. Workers will work fewer hours, have longer vacations, and retire earlier.

And these *social and economic* trends:

1. The recent rapid growth in our economy is likely to continue.

2. The gaps between the affluent and deprived in this country and between the "developed" and "Developing" nations will become greater.

3. Domestic and international social problems will become more complex and difficult to solve.

4. Institutions will grow larger and more centralized.

5. Government will increase in size and power.

With these *educational* trends:

1. More people will attend school for a greater number of years.

2. Over 25 million adults are now participating in adult education; the number, as well as the proportion of the total population, will increase.

3. Education is emerging as a major economic factor.

4. Federal investment will increase and the federal policy role become more important.

5. New techniques and methods are now developing.

6. New concepts and curricula of education are emerging slowly.

From which Liveright deduces these *implications for adult education:*

1. A lifelong, integrated program and process of learning must be developed to make continual participation acceptable and expected.

2. Students of all ages must "learn how to learn," rather than merely be taught.

3. Self-study must be emphasized, with opportunities and materials provided to encourage it.

4. Educational programs, materials, and facilities that are relevant, accessible, meaningful, and important to all social classes must be developed.

5. Computer technology and the mass media must be harnessed to the expanding needs of continuing education.

6. Adults must be provided with rewards, benefits, stimulation, support, and financial assistance.

7. The maximum use of the research and scientific skills of university faculty, as well as the skills of those who have joined industry and government, must be made in solving societal and personal problems emanating from the above trends.

8. New institutional forms providing flexibility, visibility, relevance, and accessibility must be developed to overcome past aversions, reluctance, and opposition to continuing education.[59]

Knowles identifies the following *"characteristics and dynamics" of adult education* as a field:

59. Liveright, 1968, pp. 7–16.

1. The adult education field is highly expansive and flexible.

2. It is becoming a multidimensional social system (with an institutional, a subject-matter, a geographical, and a personnel dimension).

3. The adult education field is a highly interactive social system.

4. It is developing a distinctive curriculum and methodology.

5. Adult education is becoming an increasingly delineated field of study and practice.[60]

He then proceeds to make these *predictions* based on present trends and assumptions:

1. The size of the "student body" of adult education will expand.

2. The educational level of this student body will continue to rise.

3. The resources and facilities for the education of adults will gradually expand.

4. The curriculum and methodology of adult education will become increasingly differentiated from those designed for children and youth.

5. There will be a rapid expansion in the body of knowledge about the education of adults.

6. The role of the adult educator will be increasingly differentiated from other roles, and training for this role will become more specialized.[61]

There is general agreement among the social analysts, as reported in the literature of adult education, that the last third of the twentieth century will witness the emergence of continuing education as a major force in our society.

60. Knowles, 1962, pp. 249–56.
61. *Ibid.*, pp. 269–72.

5 Contemporary Issues in Higher Adult Education

Adult education has been emerging as an identifiable field of social practice for almost 50 years. It now appears to have established an identity and to be moving into a phase of organization as a social system.

This phase is characterized by efforts to achieve policy clarification, define the roles of subsystems, achieve coordination through a communications network, establish norms and standards, provide for the continuing development of its personnel, relate to similar movements in other countries, and gain the understanding and support of the public. Higher adult education traditionally has taken a role of leadership in the total field's emergence.

The unresolved issues confronting higher adult education have been implicit in the preceding pages. Here they are made explicit and organized into a conceptual framework that becomes, in effect, higher adult education's agenda for leadership in the next decade.

NATIONAL ISSUES

1. What should be the role of institutions of higher education in the education of adults? What are the adult educational objectives and constituencies uniquely appropriate to colleges and universities as distinguished from those of other agencies?

> Should there be a national policy (or consensus) regarding the adult educational role of colleges and universities? If so, what should it be, and how should it be evolved? Or is society better served by encouraging local institutions to define their own roles?

> If there should be no national policy, should local institutions be provided models or guidelines to assist in defining their roles? Would society be better served if the different institutions (public, private; urban, state-wide; universities, liberal arts colleges, community colleges) defined their roles as different but complementary?

2. What should be the role of the federal government in higher adult education? [1]

> How can federal participation best achieve social advance? By providing direct services, such as collecting and disseminating data, sponsoring research, and giving leadership to national policy conferences, to the field?

1. For a detailed list of proposals by the U.S. Office of Education for handling these issues, see Liveright, 1968, pp. 114–33.

43

By providing financial support: (a) for basic continuing programs or for special projects; (b) for innovation or for established programs; (c) for state-desired services or for federally-desired services; (d) for students or for institutions?

How should the federal government be organized to perform its role? What coordination and control of federal activities should be established, and how?

What should be the relationships between federal agencies, state and local governments, and operating institutions in implementing federal programs:

Detailed federal program planning vs. broad program guidelines?

Broad national programs vs. local program needs?

General institutional grants vs. individual project requests?

Fund allocations through state governmental agencies vs. direct grants to operating institutions?

Fund allocations through local umbrella organizations vs. direct grants to operating institutions?

Program design, fund allocations, and supervision through regional federal offices vs. direct responsibility from Washington?

3. How can the national associations best relate to one another? Should the individuals and institutions concerned with higher adult education speak with one voice, or is there added strength in a chorus organized around special interests? What should be the role of national associations in advancing the field of higher adult education?

4. What coordination or joint planning should be sought at the national and regional levels? Through what mechanisms?

5. What stimulative, informational, research, and planning services are best provided at the national level? Through what mechanisms?

6. How can the supply of trained professional workers for the field be most rapidly and effectively enlarged nationally?

7. How can more effective international relations be achieved on the part of our national higher adult education enterprise: with international organizations such as UNESCO, with other national systems of higher adult education, with overseas developmental and growth endeavors?

8. How can the new meaning of lifelong learning be interpreted to the public, to the policy makers of higher education, and to the educators of youth so that its implications for their respective areas of responsibility are fully understood?

STATE ISSUES

1. How can each state organize its adult educational resources most effectively to identify and meet the higher adult educational needs of its people and institutions?

Is there a more or less standard mechanism for state-wide planning (such as the state plan framework set up by Title I of the Higher Education Act) which ought to be urged on all states?

Are there differential roles for general and cooperative extension? If so, what models of collaboration can be recommended? If not, what models of unification can be recommended?

2. What financial aid and supportive services can best be provided by state governments? Through what mechanisms?

3. How can more effective relationships be established between state higher adult education enterprises, regional organizations, and the federal government?

INSTITUTIONAL ISSUES

1. How shall an institution for higher education identify and define its role in adult education? How can it determine its target clientele and select the appropriate educational services to be rendered? How can guidelines be provided local institutions for this clarifying process?

2. How can an institution for higher education best organize to perform this role? Can tested models for institutions of different types be provided local institutions to aid them in improving their organizational structures?

3. Should the curriculum and methodology of higher adult education be based on different assumptions and concepts than the regular programs for youth? How shall these assumptions and concepts be formulated, disseminated, and adopted?

4. Should the quality of programs (and the evaluation of the students in them) be assessed according to different standards from those used to assess the regular programs for youth? If so, how should these differential criteria and standards be formulated, disseminated, and adopted?

5. Is it essential to effective program development for an adult clientele that the constituents be involved in the planning of programs affecting them? If so, what mechanisms for involving the clientele in program development can be created which do not conflict with the already established university decision-making machinery?

6. How can the personnel policies and practices of higher adult education be improved:

Concerning criteria and control in faculty selection?

Concerning compensation, status, and other rewards of the adult educational faculty vis-à-vis the regular faculty?

In developing nuclei of full-time faculties for adult education?

Regarding in-service training for faculties?

7. How can the financial policies and practices of higher adult education be improved:

In budgetary philosophy (profit vs. subsidy, etc.)?

In standardization of accounting and reporting procedures?

In balancing project operation under grants with long-run program development?

In obtaining greater understanding about and commitment to extension's financial needs by university administrators?

8. How can an institution for higher education best relate to other institutions providing services in this field, including corporations, government agencies, professional associations, voluntary organizations, and proprietary schools? Can guidelines or models for such relationships be provided to local institutions to aid them in making decisions?

THE ULTIMATE ISSUE

The ultimate issue confronting higher adult education in the 1970s is that of survival. The pressure of societal need for massive, relevant, and dynamic programs for the continuing education of adults is becoming so great that if it cannot be satisfied within our institutions of higher education, it will be satisfied outside them. University adult educators are increasingly apprehensive over competition from big business. In the words of Robert J. Pitchell, executive director of the National University Extension Association:

> The educational establishment for all its size and strength cannot help but take notice of the size and strength of the corporate Goliaths which have entered the field of education. Xerox, Time, General Electric, I.B.M., Raytheon, R.C.A., C.B.S., Minnesota Mining and Manufacturing Co., Litton Industries, I.T.T., Lear Siegler, and Westinghouse have all taken on one or more educational activities which go beyond the manufacture of materials and equipment or in-service training programs for their own employees.[2]

During the past few years, scores of profit and nonprofit corporations, such as the National Training Laboratories-Institute of Applied Behavioral Sciences, the Sterling Institute, Leadership Resources, Inc., Eselen Institute, the American Management Association, and Kairos Institute, have found a thriving market for programs in leadership development, human relations training, business management, and other fields of study traditionally in the university domain.

Clearly, the survival of higher adult education as a university function is threatened unless university policy-makers successfully resolve the issues now confronting them.

2. Report to the Adult Education Committee of the American Council on Education, 1967, p. IV–32.

A A Suggested System of Classification for Issues of Policy and Practice in Higher Adult Education

I. National policies and practices
  A. The role of higher adult education in national policy
    (For example: There should be a White House conference every five years to reassess the needs and resources of higher adult education as an instrument for achieving national goals.)
  B. The role of the federal government in higher adult education
    1. In providing services
    2. In providing financial support
    3. In establishing relationships with states and institutions
  C. The role of national educational associations in higher adult education
    1. General associations
    2. Special interest associations
  D. The role of American higher adult education in international relations
II. State policies and practices
  A. Organization
    1. Coordination and planning
      a) Among public institutions
      b) Among public and private institutions
    2. Relationship to regional and national bodies
  B. Financial support
  C. Services to institutions
III. Institutional policies and practices
  A. Purpose and goals
    (For example: Houle's formulation: (1) It should restrict itself to complex subject matter; (2) it should be a pioneer; (3) it should train leaders; (4) it should collaborate with other agencies; (5) it should master adult education as a field of knowledge.)
    1. As to objectives in terms of educational outcomes
    2. As to clientele
    3. As to contributions to society
  B. Organization
    1. Coordination of adult educational services and activities
    2. Relationship with established schools and departments
    3. Status of adult education unit in the administrative structure
    4. Involvement of the constituency in decision-making
  C. Personnel
    1. Selection, training, responsibilities, compensation, and status of the administrators
    2. Selection, training, responsibilities, compensation, and status of the faculty members
  D. Curriculum and services
    1. Unique principles for the organization of the adult curriculum
    2. Unique instructional technology for adult students
    3. Unique criteria of evaluation of adult programs

47

E. Financing
   1. Budgetary philosophy
   2. Accounting and reporting procedures
   3. Relationship of grant projects to on-going program
   4. Differential financial practices for adult clientele
F. Relationships with other institutions
   1. In planning
   2. In program operations
G. Professional training for adult educators
   1. Graduate education
   2. In-service education

B Suggested Operational Objectives and Evaluative Questions

CONCERNING ORGANIZATIONAL CLIMATE AND STRUCTURE

Objectives	*Evaluative Questions*
To maintain a dynamic policy base for adult education in our institution.	Does the present policy statement convey a clear commitment to adult education? Does it define purposes relevant to contemporary needs and conditions? Does it accord adequate status and influence to the adult education function? Has it been reviewed by the policy-makers within a reasonable period of time?
To assure participation of all relevant parties in policy-making and management of the adult education operation.	What would be the ideal organizational structure for this enterprise? Where does the present structure fall short of this ideal? Are all the committees' functions clearly stated and understood by their members? Do the committees function well as groups? Do they accept responsibility as groups, think cooperatively, and make decisions efficiently? Are the individual committee members personally involved in the organization? Do they subscribe to its objectives? Do they give active service? Are staff services to committees adequate? Are notices of meetings sent in time? Are adequate records kept? Is there follow-up on decisions? Are the committees working on significant matters? Are they being challenged to be creative? Are the committees' memberships representative of all parties with a stake in the program?
To provide staff service to the program at a high level of excellence.	Is the staff personnel adequate in number to the needs of the program? Are all necessary staff services performed? Is there adequate differentiation and yet flexibility in role definitions? Is there a spirit of teamwork? Are staff members involving participants and committee members in sharing responsibilities and rewards imaginatively? Are there good working conditions, adequate salaries, and sound personnel policies and practices?

Appendix B is from *The Modern Practice of Adult Education*, by Malcolm S. Knowles (New York: Association Press, forthcoming).

49

| *Objectives* | *Evaluative Questions* |

Are staff members paying adequate attention to their own continuing self-development? Are they good models for continuing learners?

To maintain an institutional atmosphere that is conducive to adult learning.

Are participants treated with warmth, dignity, and respect at all points of contact?

Is the rich experience of participants used to the fullest extent in policy-making, planning, management, learning, and evaluation?

Do we know in what ways the participants feel they are treated as more and less adult in their experience with us?

CONCERNING ASSESSMENT OF NEEDS AND INTERESTS

To maintain an up-to-date inventory of the individual needs and interests, organizational needs, and community needs our program should be serving.

Have surveys of these three types of needs (and interests) been made within a reasonable period?

Is some individual or group taking responsibility for sensing changing needs and interests from contacts with community leaders, the mass media, and professional literature?

Are the techniques we are using for the collection and analysis of data about needs and interests keeping pace with advancing survey technology?

Do the assessed needs include predicted future needs as well as identified present needs?

CONCERNING DEFINITINON OF PURPOSES AND OBJECTIVES

To maintain an up-to-date statement of purposes which will provide direction, coherence, and relevance to the program.

Has the present statement of purpose been reviewed within a reasonable period of time?

Does it delineate clearly the role of adult education in the institution?

Does it specify clearly the long-range goals and constituency?

Does it express a philosophy of education that is congruent with modern knowledge about adults as learners?

Are the purposes significant and relevant in the light of contemporary conditions?

To develop and promulgate operational and educational objectives that provide clear guidance in current program development, operation, and evaluation.

Have the objectives been reviewed within a reasonable period of time?

Are they clearly related to assessed needs?

Are they stated in terms of measurable outcomes?

Are they known, understood, and accepted by policy-makers, leaders and instructors, and participants?

Objectives	*Evaluative Questions*

Concerning Program Design

To maintain a sense of artistic quality in the program design.

Is a sense of *line* provided by a dynamic theme, activity sequences, and time schedule?

Does an interesting *space pattern* emerge from the rhythm of activities, varying depth of activities, control of size of activities, etc.?

Is the *tone* of the program one of warmth, varying emphases, and personalization?

Is the *color* of the program bright and warm, as conveyed by publicity materials, the arrangement and decoration of physical facilities, and the personnel?

Is the *texture* of the program interesting, rich, and functional? Does the design make use of a variety of formats for learning appropriately?

Does the program design have a sense of *unity*, balance, and integration?

To maintain a program that serves the purposes and meets the needs for which it was intended.

Are the activities in the program design consistent with the institution's purposes? Do they achieve these purposes?

Are the activities based on the stated objectives? Do they carry out these objectives?

Is the program design adequate in scope and emphases?

Is the design flexible enough to adapt quickly to changing needs and conditions?

Is provision made for participants to influence the program design?

Concerning Program Operation

To provide the highest quality faculty of leaders and instructors possible.

Are the criteria of selection clear, adequate, and in keeping with principles of andragogy? Are they applied?

Is the compensation on a professional basis? Is it competitive with other institutions?

Do new instructors and leaders receive adequate orientation and individual coaching?

Do the entire faculty receive adequate in-service training and supervision? Do they perceive it as a program of continuing self-directed self-development?

Is the performance of faculty members periodically assessed?

To provide physical facilities that make an environment conducive to adult learning.

Are the meeting rooms adequate in number, size, flexibility, comfort, and attractiveness?

Are leaders and instructors helped to arrange rooms for maximum informality and interaction?

Objectives	Evaluative Questions
	Are the lighting, ventilation, and storage facilities adequate?
	Are the physical facilities maintained in good condition?
	Is there adequate instructional equipment? Is it properly safeguarded and maintained in good condition? Is the faculty given sufficient help in using it well?
	Is provision made for the replacement or renewal of physical facilities before they deteriorate?
	Are the space and equipment used as close to capacity as is practicable?
	Are the office facilities adequate, attractive, and efficient?
To provide administrative services that facilitate the educational objectives of the program.	Are the office services adequate in quantity and quality? Is correspondence answered promptly? Is filing efficient?
	Are inquiries and registrations handled promptly, courteously, and with dignity?
	Are records accurate, as comprehensive as necessary, as simple as practicable, and accessible?
	Is adequate educational counseling service available to participants?
	Are participants given personalized attention during registration and opening sessions? Are veteran participants used as hosts and hostesses?
To provide promotion and public relations services that will advance the objectives of the program.	Is the desired clientele clearly defined?
	Is the present promotion program recruiting this clientele?
	Is the promotion campaign adequately planned and efficiently carried out?
	Do the promotion materials accurately reflect the quality and spirit of the program? Do they establish the proper expectations and climate for learning?
	Are the various media used appropriately and effectively?
	Are the results of the various elements of promotion evaluated adequately?
	Is the program adequately interpreted to the public?
To provide adequate financial resources and procedures to maintain a high quality program.	Are the financial goals adequate and realistic in terms of the program's objectives?
	Are the program goals reflected accurately in the financial budget?
	Does the budget provide sufficient guidance, flexibility, and control?

Objectives   *Evaluative Questions*

Are adequate financial procedures and records maintained?

Are the financial policies clear, realistic, and in keeping with the nature of the clientele and the spirit of the institution?

Are all possible sources of income being drawn upon?

Is the financial experience of the program adequately reported and interpreted?

CONCERNING PROGRAM EVALUATION

To obtain information that will promote continuous program improvement.

Are the purposes of any proposed evaluation clear and understood by all parties who will be involved?

Are plans for evaluation made as part of the program planning process?

Are realistic priorities set which will result in the most important improvements?

Are all parties who will be affected by evaluation represented in planning it?

Are the most efficient and reliable means used for getting the desired data?

Are the data adequately analyzed and the findings fed back into the planning process?

Are those from whom data were obtained informed about the findings and the use that is made of them?

C Guidelines for Member Institutions: The Structure of University Extension

There is no single right way for a university to organize itself to meet its commitment to extension. Both the history of past endeavors and the aspirations for future growth cause every institution to shape and reshape its own way of work. However, the National University Extension Association believes that certain guidelines should be observed:

1. Extension must be accepted as a primary function of the university.

2. Governing boards, central policy makers and administrators, and faculties of the universities must understand the goals of the total institutional program of extension. This program must reflect the level of quality of the university itself. The institutional commitment must be made clear. Adequate resources must be allocated.

3. Policies governing extension must provide for the recruitment and retention of a quality staff, with an institutional reward system that provides rank, tenure, and the other essentials to perform extension teaching, research, and administrative tasks well. Those engaged in extension must be recognized throughout the university as having a clear professional status and respected career line.

4. The university must plan carefully and comprehensively for its extension program.

5. The entire extension effort must be coordinated within the university. Strong leadership in the administrative structure of the university is required to secure this coordination. A comprehensive approach to some of the complex problems extension is asked to deal with becomes impossible without university-wide coordination.

6. The size, nature, and depth of involvement of the very large and heterogeneous extension student body, and other clientele, should be analyzed constantly. This evaluation should guide extension policy-makers and other administrators in formulating institutional commitments in terms of the needs of the individuals and the segments of society the institution seeks to serve.

7. Extension should not be expected to operate on a self-supporting basis. When extension must be self-supporting it mostly will serve well only the few who can afford to pay for it, and it will not serve at all the many whose needs are of greatest concern. Extension must have consistent financial support from university funds to be effective in meeting community and social needs.

8. The university must be creative in adapting program content and format to specific objectives, in finding new equivalents for traditional requirements, and in the methods required to meet its extension commitment. These conditions can be met with full respect for university standards of quality.

9. More state-wide, regional, and national programs of extension must be developed. Universities should plan jointly to meet pressing needs and to develop the appropriate mechanisms and resources for special purposes.

Appendix C is from "College and University Extension: NUEA Position Paper, The Structure of University Extension" *NUEA Spectator* (February-March 1968), pp. 8-9.

10. The university must be prepared to cooperate with governmental agencies—local, state, and national—and with private organizations in the conduct of educational programs essential to the achievement of its social goals. Within the framework of this partnership government and private organizations should pay the cost of specific programs and also should provide continuing financial support to develop the capability of the university to provide the services.

University Adult Education:
A Selected Bibliography,
1968

Publishers or original sources for the documents abstracted in this bibliography are given with each citation. *AC* and *ED* numbers have no subject significance; they are accession numbers used by the ERIC Clearinghouse on Adult Education and are useful when corresponding with ERIC/AE about any of the documents so marked.

All documents listed by *ED* number, e.g., ED 010 679, may be purchased from the ERIC Document Reproduction Service in microfiche or hardcopy reproductions. Microfiche is a 4 by 6-inch film sheet containing up to 70 pages of text in a reduction ratio of 18:1 with an eye-readable title; it may be read on any standard microfiche reader. Hardcopy reproductions are 6 by 8 inches and can be read without magnification. Only those documents with *ED* numbers may be ordered. For further information write to: ERIC Document Reproduction Service, 4936 Fairmont Avenue, Bethesda, Maryland 20014.

All publications of the Center for the Study of Liberal Education for Adults (CSLEA) may be obtained from the Syracuse University Press, Box 8, University Station, Syracuse, New York 13210.

Adolfson, L. H., and others. *Today's Critical Needs and University Extension.* Association of State Universities and Land-Grant Colleges, Washington, D.C., 1961. 11 pp. AC 001 858

The position paper outlines the basic characteristics, methods, requirements, and mission of university extension education. The extension service should be related to all segments of the university, extending its resources to all people. The philosophy of university extension is to make itself as useful as possible to the total society, by identifying public problems, needs, interpreting these to the university, and focusing university skills, and resources to solve them. A variety of methods in education are utilized, such as specialized residential instruction, applied research, evening classes, radio and television courses, publications, and correspondence study. Among changes in society that require maximum involvement of colleges and universities in extension education are growth of population, increase in standard of living and leisure time, and urbanization. Program areas demanding intensive action include continuing education for the technical, professional and postgraduate, citizenship training, retirement orientation, family life, international and labor education. Available from the Association of State Universities and Land-Grant Colleges, 1785 Massachusetts Avenue, N.W., Washington, D.C. 20036.

This selected bibliography on university adult education was prepared by the ERIC Clearinghouse on Adult Education and the Syracuse University Library of Continuing Education.

Adult Education Association of the U.S.A., Commission on Architecture. *Architecture for Adult Education.* Chicago, Ill., 1953. 74 pp.

A graphic guide for planning physical facilities for adult education. Photographs, floor plans, and discussion of health centers, religious buildings, buildings for industry, elementary schools, high schools, college buildings, audiovisual facilities, libraries, recreational buildings, community centers, and buildings especially for adult education.

————. *Federal Support for Adult Education; A Directory of Programs and Services.* Washington, D.C., 1966. 119 pp. ED 010 679

This directory groups federal adult education programs and services alphabetically by administering agencies and lists, wherever applicable, (1) program title, (2) nature and purpose of the program, (3) eligible groups and organizations, (4) amount (where possible) and nature of the funds or other assistance, (5) printed materials available, and (8) additional comments. The Departments of Agriculture; Commerce; Defense; Health, Education, and Welfare; Housing and Urban Development; the Interior; Justice; Labor; and State and various independent executive agencies, including those reporting directly to the President, are represented. The document includes a list of legislation and a list of selected publications. Bibliography pp. 110–11.

American Association of Junior Colleges. *Junior College Directory, 1965.* Washington, D.C., 1965. 50 pp.

Directory of information on public and private junior colleges. Alphabetical list, enrollment data by institution, various summaries, and descriptive tables.

Aspen Institute for Humanistic Studies. *Annual Report, 1965.* Aspen, Colo., 1965. 33 pp.

The 1965 Aspen report reviews the Aspen Executive Program, the Aspen Award ceremony honoring dancer Martha Graham, art activities, public programs (lectures, etc.), planning conferences, programs in the sciences and humanities, conferences on design and architecture, and complementary programs. Contributors to the Institute, members of the Aspen Society of Fellows, and new members are listed. Photographs and descriptions of facilities are included. Supplement lists conferences and participants.

Association of University Evening Colleges. *Salary Survey of Administrative Personnel.* Norman, Okla., 1965. 16 pp.

Characteristics of AUEC member institutions and their evening divisions and of evening-college staff are summarized from questionnaires completed by 555 individuals and 111 institutions. Evening-college salary scales are correlated with institutional data on type of control, religious affiliation, size of classes, financial policy, course offerings, credit or noncredit programs, geographical locations, and attitudes of other institutional officials toward the evening division and with personal data (age, length of service, degrees held, etc.) on evening-college administrative personnel.

Bailey, Stephen K. "Urban Decision-Making; The University's Role." In *Political Backgrounds of Adult Education,* edited by Thomas Cummings. CSLEA, Boston, 1967. 14 pp. ED 011 364

The author examines the various ways in which the university can and should influence urban decision-making. The central university role is sensitizing the decision-makers and the citizens to human misery, such as bigotry, squalor, disease, ugliness, poverty, and ignorance. Long-range roles are, pinpointing the problems urban decision-makers should deal with, discovering the root laws of human behavior and finding answers to problems according to these laws. Short-range roles include providing technical advice and educating urban decision-makers.

Bebout, John E. "University Services to the Urban Community." *American Behavioral Scientist*, February 1963. 19 pp. AC 000 070

This essay explores the nature of the relationship between university and community that characterizes urban extension. Distinctions and similarities between cooperative extension and the urban extension method are noted. Basic requisites of effective urban extension projects—appropriateness, significance, and avoidance of waste and duplication—are explained. Fundamental areas of service are outlined: a comprehensive clearinghouse, counseling and consultation, sponsorship of policy conferences and seminars, special education in urban affairs, dissemination of general education and public information, demonstration projects, and active support of communication among groups and individuals who shape urban policy. Six closely related tasks—adjustment of urban dwellers to changing environments, community development, neighborhood organization, area coordination, application of special-area expertise, and liaison between universities and the users of knowledge—are delineated. Suggested training policy, notably the recruitment and training of volunteers and subprofessionals, and means of cooperation and division of labor and money are discussed. Document includes notes for designing a master plan for urban extension in the New York metropolitan area.

Benne, Kenneth. "Adult Education in the University; A Primitive Look at the University System." *Journal of Higher Education*, November 1956. 6 pp. AC 001 197

Discusses relationships and conflicting interests among elements of university social systems, i.e., academic personnel, administrative personnel, and categories of students (graduates, undergraduates, and adult extension participants). University extension programs are shown as reflected primarily in the needs, concerns, and interests of the wider society.

Blackwell, Gordon W. "Community Needs and Higher Continuing Education." In *The Continuing Task; Reflection on Purpose in Higher Continuing Education*. Center for the Study of Liberal Education for Adults, Boston, 1967. 11 pp. AC 001 065

Urban universities and continuing higher education may help meet the needs of the changing urban community by reorganizing its continuing education activities to meet constantly changing needs. Universities, geared more directly to social action than 15 years ago, are entering into creative partnership with the government, industry, and civic organizations.

————. "The University and Continuing Education in the Future." In *Today and Tomorrow; Three Essays on Adult Education in the Future*. CSLEA Notes and Essays on Education for Adults, number 34. Center for the Study of Liberal Education for Adults, Chicago, 1961.

A look at the social and organizational changes occurring in the contemporary American scene, with focus on three elements of rapid change with which education will be faced in the immediate future: (1) rapid shift from a rural to urban way of life; (2) development of fused and linear cities; (3) general massification of society. Implications of these trends for continuing education are discussed, with four areas selected for special consideration. The first is alumni education which must begin on the campus in the undergraduate program, with information provided the students on the kinds of continuing education programs which the institution will provide. The second area is educational guidance centers for mature women. The third area is education for the aging. The last area for attention is that of continuing education and community problems. Continuing education must be closely related to technical problems facing local and state governments as the future of American society becomes increasingly complex.

Boone, E. J., and Ferguson, C. M., eds. *Changing Dimensions in Agriculture and Home Economics; Impact on Cooperative Extension Administration.* National Agricultural Extension Center for Advanced Study, Madison, Wis., 1962. 94 pp.

Various authors consider some of the basic trends in agriculture and home economics which will shape the future problems of agricultural extension programming and administration. The authors deal with substantive changes and the implications for program, staff training, methods, and administrative practice and from national and state viewpoints. List of publications of the National Agricultural Extension Center for Advanced Study.

Briley, John Marshall. *Master Plan for State Policy in Higher Education.* Ohio Board of Regents, Columbus, Ohio, 1966. 169 pp. ED 014 273

A comprehensive plan for public higher education in Ohio is presented as a guide to implementing and continuing the policy of open access to state-assisted institutions of higher education for all Ohio residents who graduate from high school. In this plan, the Ohio Board of Regents, which is the state-wide planning and coordinating agency for public policy in higher education, gives attention to (1) the roles of each of the existing public higher education institutions, (2) current status and future needs for specific undergraduate programs, (3) professional education, (4) graduate study and research, (5) enrollment distributions and priorities for new institutions and additional facilities, and (6) special areas of library services, educational radio and television, continuing education, teaching hospitals, student assistance, and retirement and fringe benefits. A total of 126 recommendations and policy statements are supported by chapters which include background information and findings of the studies conducted by the regents.

British Columbia, University of, Vancouver, University Extension. *Continuing Education in the Professions; A Symposium (University of British Columbia, October 25, 1961).* 1962. 62 pp.

Papers on continuing education in the professions by Roby Kidd and Paul Sheats, with extensive commentary by a panel of experts. Kidd discusses the nature of a profession and the contributions of the professional man in society, drawing implications for professional education and stressing the importance of liberal education. Sheats, using the explosive growth of professional continuing education at the University of California as example, discusses types of programs in university extension, again with emphasis on reaching professional people with liberal education.

Burch, Glen. *Challenge to the University; An Inquiry into the University's Responsibility for Adult Education.* CSLEA Notes and Essays on Education for Adults, number 35. Center for the Study of Liberal Education for Adults, Chicago, 1961. 79 pp.

An examination, published in 1961, of the entire range of policy problems in university adult education, with special attention to its "unassimilated" service function. Many illustrations of current trends are presented from programs of various universities.

Burkett, J. E., and Ruggiers, Paul G., eds. *Bachelor of Liberal Studies; Development of a Curriculum at the University of Oklahoma.* Center for the Study of Liberal Education for Adults, Boston, 1965. 117 pp. AC 000 532

A program leading to the Bachelor of Liberal Studies (BLS) for adult, part-time students was conceived and implemented at the University of Oklahoma between 1957 and 1965. The program is designed to surmount difficulties posed by rigid course and residence requirements, scheduling, and undergraduate-oriented instruction. By giving special entrance examinations, holding brief highly concentrated seminars, furnishing individual reading lists, consultations, and further examinations, and organizing content around "central learnings which bear on the central problems of the twentieth century," instructors can engage the interest of adults and satisfactorily evaluate their progress. Independent study in the three broad areas—humanities, natural sciences, and social sciences—is followed by interarea studies directed toward an interdisciplinary view of particular problems and questions. All BLS candidates must complete four independent study courses and four seminars, but each candidate can complete his total program at the pace that best suits his own previous education, academic capability, and time available for study. (Conclusions and implications are discussed. The document includes typical schedules and seminar topics, reading lists, enrollment statistics, five tables, and a bibliography.

Burns, Hobert W., ed. *Sociological Backgrounds of Adult Education.* CSLEA Notes and Essays on Education for Adults, number 41. Center for the Study of Liberal Education for Adults, Chicago, 1964. 178 pp.

Background information on social trends presented by five sociologists to a conference of university adult educators. Burton Clark on the implications of the growth of research and development; Robert Havighurst on changing status and roles during the life span; Henry Sheldon on adult population trends. John Johnstone presents data from his 1961 study of participation in adult education and projects participation rates into the future. Introduction by Hobert Burns and extensive comments by the adult educators are included.

Bye, Carl R. "Instructional Standards for Adult Education Programs." *Conference on New Directions for Adult Education (Syracuse University, April 18–20, 1958)*, pp. 33–36.

Considers major advantages and disadvantages of evening college learning situations in the light of the problem of maintaining course standards.

California, University of, Berkeley; University Extension. *University of California Extension in a Decade of Transition; A Report to the Combined Academic Senate Committee on University Extension Covering the Years 1952–62.* 1963. 44 pp.

An overview of the efforts of the Extension Division of the University of California to provide continuing education, underscoring the changing nature of extension clientele, the variety of demands upon a state university system, and the growing social urgency for more rapid dissemination of new knowledge. Trends noted are: (1) the rise of the professional extension administrator; (2) development of numerous certificate programs; (3) expansion of publishing activities; (4) film production based on the curriculum; (5) international programs at the highest professional levels; (6) dissemination of research findings to top echelon national groups; (7) expanded correspondence programs, involving more offerings on the upper division and professional levels; (8) expanded scope in music extension and theater; (9) broad conferences; (10) rise in level of extension services to unions; (11) new emphasis on executive education programs; (12) emphasis on extremely advanced professional courses in engineering and sciences. Future predictions include a shift to postgraduate courses with less emphasis on parallel degree credit courses; an increase in the number and nature of sequential programs in the liberal arts which involve new formats and new combinations of subject matter; no expansion of degree credit courses; increase in the trend toward decentralization of extension administration; strengthening of the faculty-extension relationships; programmed instruction to replace many of the traditional methods; an increase in government and institutional contracts and grants.

————. University-wide Academic Senate Committee on University Extension. *The New Challenge in Lifelong Learning; A Conference on the Future Role of the University in Relation to Public Service (Lake Arrowhead, California, May 9–11, 1965).* 1965. 79 pp.

Though focused on the problems of California, this report includes papers on a range of topics of general interest in university adult extension. Various authors discuss the history of agricultural and general extension in California; the appropriate role of the university in public services; the problems of enrollment and cost projections; curriculum for manpower development, for liberal education, and for use of leisure time; prospects for the future of university adult education.

Calkins, Robert D. "New Tasks for Our Universities." *Proceedings of the Annual Meeting of the National University Extension Association (47th, 1962),* pp. 23–31. 1962.

Continuing education for wiser, more effective leadership, both in professions and occupations and in public life, is viewed as a national necessity. Needs and goals are outlined, and the skills and surroundings required to promote mature learning and inquiry are indicated.

Carey, James T. *The Development of the University Evening College as Observed in Ten Urban Universities.* CSLEA Research Reports. Center for the Study of Liberal Education for Adults, Chicago, 1961. 73 pp.

A study dealing with the emergence of the university evening school on the American scene, its history, operational dynamics, and social relationships. Emphasis is on four hypotheses: (1) the tendency to develop a stable student body committed to a certain period of time; (2) the tendency to choose a dean from the academic world and to develop a full-time faculty in the evening division; (3) the tendency toward a wide selection of traditional programs; and (4) the tendency to develop a substantial amount of capital equipment. Evening colleges encourage the development of an evening student culture, with student consciousness organized around the degree programs in the evening. Typically, the dean or director comes from teaching a subject matter specialty, but there is a trend for administrators to come with professional training in adult education, and a movement to professionalize the field. The trend is also toward a regular salary schedule and tenure for evening faculty who are full-time in the evening division. In the curriculum, the tendency is toward a more complete offering of all day-time programs, with attempts to sell entire programs rather than discrete courses. A crucial element in the evening division's autonomy seems to be the number of conference centers, off-campus holdings and residential meeting places.

————. *Forms and Forces in University Adult Education.* Center for the Study of Liberal Education for Adults, Chicago, 1963. 229 pp. AC 000 676.

This report summarizes information from an extensive study of university adult education conducted through questionnaires to AUEC-NUEA institutions and a sample of liberal arts colleges, plus interviews with various officials in 18 colleges and universities. Though particularly focused on liberal adult education, this is the best and most detailed study of the range of forces which favor or impede the growth of adult education in American higher education. Following a chapter on the history of university adult education and one on the status of liberal education programming, the report explores such factors as tradition, nature of the personnel, financial arrangements, goals and objectives, the community context, etc. A model growth cycle of adult education divisions is suggested and profiles of various types of divisions are presented. Appendix 1 gives notes on the methodology used for the study. Many tables are included.

Carlin, Edward. "Whose Is the University?" *Growing Time,* pp. 38–43. CSLEA Notes and Essays on Education for Adults, number 44. Center for the Study of Liberal Education for Adults, Boston, 1964.

Three social systems in constant interaction create healthy tension in the life of the university. While not mutually exclusive, they have significant differences in their relationships to the university. These social systems are: (1) the public, composed of a broad spectrum of individuals and groups, from those who cannot name the university to those who are in constant contact; (2) the university community itself, including not only the professors, students, administrators, housekeepers but also the larger community of scholars to which they are all related; (3) the legal system of the university, including the nature of its charter, its board of control and its established sources of funds and support.

Carnegie Corporation of New York. *Public Television; A Program for Action. Report and Recommendations of the Carnegie Commission on Educational Television.* 1967. 284 pp. AC 001 426

The report of the Carnegie Commission on Educational Television proposes a nonprofit corporation for public television to receive and disburse private and government funds. It recommends increased government support of local and national program production, new facilities for live-broadcast interconnection, research and development in programing and production and in television technology and recruitment and training of specialized talent. There should be additional enabling legislation and financing through excise taxes on television receivers. The existing system (December 1966) is outlined—sponsorship (21 school, 27 state, 35 university, and 41 community stations), sources of general programing, distribution, and financial support. Characteristics of commercial and public television and their audiences are described, and the potentials of educational television discussed. Supplementary papers also discuss legal aspects, projected long-run operating costs, and the role of the Federal Communications Commission. Financial and operating reports of education television stations, July 1965–June 1966, are presented, together with data on audience sizes and occupational and educational characteristics of listeners. Document includes 35 tables, a map, and list of ETV Stations. This document is available from Bantam Books, New York, N.Y. 10016.

Center for the Study of Liberal Education for Adults. *The College and its Community; A Conference on Purpose and Direction in the Education of Adults.* CSLEA Occasional Papers, number 16. Brookline, Mass., 1968. 64 pp. AC 002 726

At a conference on the college and its community, papers were presented by leaders of universities that had participated in the "sister-college plan" for training adult educators, sponsored by the Negro College Committee on Adult Education. The University of Wisconsin has taken the lead in moving beyond its campus, with no boundaries of geography, time, methods, clientele, or subject matter. Syracuse University has recognized its community commitments by providing leadership training, pilot and innovative programs, brokerage of community resources, theater programs, social criticism, and funding from outside sources. In their programs of remedial, vocational, and continuing education at Norfolk State College, Tuskegee Institute, and Opportunities Industrialization Centers, commitment has been to the rehabilitation of the disadvantaged. Federal funds are available for programs from other sources than Title I and the Adult Education Act, such as the Office of Economic Opportunity, the Administration on Aging, and the Department of Commerce; in some cases, state and local funds may be available. We have to sell adult education on a project-by-project basis; the important thing is to conceive imaginative projects relating university resources to community needs. We must accept the commitment that continuing education and retraining are proper functions of universities.

Chicago, University of; Studies and Training Program in Continuing Education. *A Directory of Residential Continuing Education in the United States and Canada, 1963–64.* 1965. 72 pp. AC 000 802

Descriptive list of 130 residential continuing education centers in the United States and Canada in operation in 1963–1964, sponsored largely by universities but also by private organizations, churches, foundations, and government agencies. The center descriptions are arranged in alphabetical order within each state or province, and the name and address of each director is included.

Clark, Burton R. "Knowledge, Industry and Adult Competence." In *Sociological Backgrounds of Adult Education,* pp. 1–16. CSLEA Notes and Essays on Education for Adults, number 41. 1964.

The social impact of changes in knowledge and industry are discussed in terms of obsolescence generated in industry and occupations, effects of research and development on industry and higher education, and the problem of maintaining adult competence through periodic retraining and reorientation.

Clark, Harold F., and Sloan, Harold S. *Classrooms in the Factories; An Account of Educational Activities Conducted by American Industry.* 1958. 139 pp. AC 001 782

Industrial educational activities—programs in which knowledge or skills are taught according to some predetermined plan with periodic group meetings, required assignments and examinations, or some comparable means of judging achievement—are summarized in this study. Data were obtained from questionnaires, personal conferences, company brochures, and current literature. A questionnaire directed to 482 of the largest American industrial corporations brought 349 replies (72.4 percent), of which 296 (84.8 percent) reported carrying on educational activities. About half reported supplementing their own teaching staff with college professors engaged on a part-time basis. Almost all corporations offering their employees educational opportunities in universities defray at least part of the expense. Of the five divisions of subject matter mentioned in the questionnaire, orientation and managerial development programs were the most common, followed by human relations, technical and professional training, and general education. Foremen and supervisors participate most frequently, followed by junior executives and the business and professional group. Senior executives attend conferences sponsored by such organizations as the American Management Association and universities. This document is published by the Institute of Research, Fairleigh Dickinson University, and distributed by New York University Press, 32 Washington Place, N.Y.

———. *Classrooms in the Military; An Account of Education in the Armed Forces of the United States.* Institute for Instructional Improvement, Inc. Teachers College, Columbia University, New York, 1961. 166 pp. AC 001 432

The third of a series of studies concerning education outside the traditional institutions of learning, this book is comprehensive in scope. It presents the overall pattern of education in the Armed Forces of the United States, reduces details to outline form, and explains methods and practices by means of examples.

————. *Classrooms in the Stores.* Institute for Instructional Improvement, Inc. Roxbury Press, Inc., Sweet Springs, Mo., 1962. 123 pp. AC 001 781

There is little formal training carried on in retailing. Even among the 36 largest retailers studied, three reported no educational activities, and as the stores decline in size, the percentage of establishments with no formal training programs grows. The education that is carried on is restricted to three categories: (1) orientation of the rank and file of employees to store policies, (2) instruction for salespeople in techniques of salesmanship and merchandise handling, and (3) managerial-development programs in store operation. Universities offer a separate curriculum in retailing, some high schools have a work-study program in retail training, and trade associations sponsor refresher courses for executives and employees. With scant employee training, a nonexploratory type of research, and slow productivity growth, retailing has become a bottleneck in the American economy. Mechanization of such operations as accounting and packaging and the use of teaching machines to reduce the cost of training may provide a solution. Studies indicate that the gross national product could be increased if the present handicaps to purchasing were overcome by widespread employee training and exploratory research.

Clawson, M. "The Human Environment." *The New Challenge in Lifelong Learning; A Conference on the Future Role of the University in Relation to Public Service (Lake Arrowhead, California, May 9–11, 1965),* pp. 39–44.

Discusses the impact of increasing population, rising educational levels and requirements, technological change, mobility, and leisure on future needs and demand for university adult education in California.

College Entrance Examination Board. *College-Level Examination Program; Description and Uses, 1967.* Princeton, N.J., 1967. 48 pp. ED 011 616

The College-Level Examination Program which started in 1965 as a new activity of the College Entrance Examination Board has 5 aims. They are to give a national program of examinations to evaluate nontraditional college-level education including independent study and correspondence work; to stimulate colleges and universities to become more aware of the need for and the possibilities and problems of credit by examination; to enable colleges and universities to develop appropriate procedures for the placement, accreditation, and admission of transfer students; to give colleges and universities a means by which to evaluate their programs and their students' achievement; and to help adults who wish to continue their education in order to meet licensing requirements or qualify for higher positions. The booklet serves as a guide to the program and shows examples from actual tests. The examinations are available at no charge to the institutions that wish to experiment with them. The program is still in the planning stage.

Conference of Administrative Officers and Deans of Syracuse University, April 18–20, 1958. *New Directions for Adult Education.* Syracuse University Press, Syracuse, N.Y., 1959. 85 pp.

Papers presented to a conference of administrative officers and deans of Syracuse University to brief them on various aspects of university adult education. Three essays deal with adult education at Syracuse University;

others take up such problems as needs of adult students, library provision, plant requirements, role of the community colleges and problems of academic standards. A. A. Liveright comments on the papers and examines new directions in higher adult education.

Coombs, Philip H. "The University and its External Environment." In *The Changing University* edited by George H. Daigneault, pp. 24–34. Center for the Study of Liberal Education for Adults, Chicago, 1959.

The effects of rising university enrollments, the proper scope and character of the university's educational task, and pressures of the growing university research establishment upon more peripheral programs such as university adult education are discussed. Questions are raised concerning the objectives and functions of the adult education division in continuing education.

Crimi, James E. *Adult Education in the Liberal Arts College.* CSLEA Notes and Essays on Education for Adults, number 17. Center for the Study of Liberal Education for Adults, Chicago, 1957. 38 pp.

Report of a 1954 survey on adult education programs and practices of 233 liberal arts colleges (from 404 institutions returning the questionnaire). Information on: size of enrollments; distribution by size of community; type of institutional control (private and nonsectarian, Catholic, Protestant); types of programs (credit, noncredit, lecture series, correspondence, etc.); subject content; sources of teachers; benefits, problems, trends in adult education in the liberal arts colleges.

Cummings, Thomas, Jr., ed. *Political Backgrounds of Adult Education; The University in Urban Society.* CSLEA Notes and Essays on Education for Adults, number 53. Center for the Study of Liberal Education for Adults, Boston, 1967. 88 pp. AC 000 499

This monograph contains papers presented at a conference held in October 1966 sponsored jointly by University College (the Adult Education Division of Syracuse University) and the Center for the Study of Liberal Education for Adults. The following papers are included: (1) urban decision-making: the university's role; (2) urban institutions as university clients; (3) politics of university involvement in social change; (4) teaching and research: their influence in social change; and (5) educating the urban student for the urban way of life.

Cundiff, Edward. "Academic Standards in Adult Education." In *Conference on New Directions for Adult Education (Syracuse University, April 18–20, 1958)*, pp. 37–40.

Urges practical recognition, in the form of special teaching methods and more favorable instructor attitudes, of the needs, problems, and background of the adult evening student.

Dahle, Thomas L. "Report on Research Project Concerning 'Faculty Attitudes toward the Division of Continuing Education at the University of Oregon,' Eugene." Paper presented at National Seminar on Adult Education Research, Chicago, Feb. 11–13, 1968. University of Oregon, Eugene, 1968. ED 016 926

A study was undertaken at the University of Oregon to determine faculty attitudes toward the Division of Continuing Education and its activities, including such considerations as the quality of instruction in the Division's credit courses, the rigor of grading, and the quality of the student it serves. Faculty members were also queried as to their view of the relationship between the Division of Continuing Education and the primary function of a university, and data were obtained on age, sex, academic discipline, years of college teaching, academic rank, and major occupation (teacher, researcher, or administrator). Usable questionnaires were returned by 130 respondents. Favorable attitudes correlated significantly with sex (women), discipline (professional schools), age (older faculty), and rank (associate professors), but not with the other variables. There was a slight tendency, apparently arising from insufficient information, to question the quality of instruction in the Division of Continuing Education. A need for further research and improved public relations is seen.

Daigneault, George H., ed. *The Changing University; A Report on the Seventh Annual Leadership Conference.* Center for the Study of Liberal Education for Adults, Chicago, 1959. 64 pp.

Papers on the changing environment in American higher education presented to a conference of university adult educators, including discussion of each paper by the participants. Nicholas Demerath discusses problems caused by the growth and increased complexity of universities; Philip Coombs examines the external demands on the university for increased quantity and quality in higher education, with reference to the problems of financial support; and Thomas McConnell discusses the growing elaboration and differentiation of functions in higher education.

————. *Decision Making in the University Evening Colleges; The Role of the Resident Department Chairman.* CSLEA Research Reports. Center for the Study of Liberal Education for Adults, Chicago, 1963. 70 pp.

Conclusions and descriptive information from a doctoral dissertation on decision-making processes prevalent in university evening colleges. Four publicly-supported institutions and six private, nonsectarian institutions were studied. The relation of departmental objectives to evening college objectives, arrangements for selecting and assigning faculty, patterns of authority and responsibility, and approaches to evaluating departmental evening programs are discussed.

DeCrow, Roger. *Ability and Achievement of Evening College and Extension Students.* CSLEA Reports. Center for the Study of Liberal Education for Adults, Chicago, 1959. 13 pp.

An analysis of a number of studies comparing undergraduate college students with adult university extension students in learning ability and academic achievement. In the context of credit courses at the university, the only area in which a comparison would be relevant, there is considerable evidence that adult students are equal or perhaps slightly superior to undergraduate students in learning *performance*. Without exception in the groups tested adults have shown equal or superior learning *ability*. Undocumented assertions that evening college and extension classes are inferior must be checked against these facts. Bibliography pp. 12–13.

————. *Administrative Practices in University Evening Colleges.* CSLEA Reports. Center for the Study of Liberal Education for Adults, Chicago, 1962. 74 pp.

This report of a 1961 survey of 100 member institutions of the Association of University Evening Colleges gives detailed information on administrative practices in evening colleges. Data on such topics as number and size of evening colleges; types of organizational structure; proportions of work devoted to credit, noncredit, certificate, and other programs; time and length of classes; admission policies and student services provided; tuition and fees; faculty arrangements, orientation and compensation practices; size and salaries of administrative staffs. Includes questionnaire and a list of basic information sources in university adult education.

————. *Growing Time.* CSLEA Notes and Essays on Education For Adults, number 44. Center for the Study of Liberal Education for Adults, Boston, 1964. 82 pp.

A selection of papers by various authors presented over the years to the Michigan State University Seminars on University Adult Education. The papers are organized in three sections: (1) social trends as they affect university adult education with papers by Howard Higman, Milton Stern, and John S. Diekhoff; (2) the nature of the university, including papers by Edward Carlin, Paul Miller, and Thomas Hamilton; (3) the tasks of the adult educator with papers by Thurman White, Malcolm Knowles, Julius Nolte, and John Friesen.

Demerath, Nicholas J. "The Changing Character of the University." In *The Changing University,* edited by George H. Daigneault, pp. 5–23. Center for the Study of Liberal Education for Adults, Chicago, 1959.

Tensions and stresses within the university are described, including the growing conflict of interest between faculties and university administrators. Major policy issues affecting the future quality of university adult education, e.g., educational structures and patterns of recognition for faculty, are raised.

Deters, Richard T. "Equal under Law; The Rights of Part-Time College Students." In *The Next Twenty-five Years; Proceedings of the Annual Meeting of the Association of University Evening Colleges (25th, 1963),* pp. 46–52.

The adult night student, like the day adolescent, is a human being with all a person's gifts, privileges, and rights; and his advanced education is in the national interest. There are those who think that it is more important to prepare scholars, teachers, and scientists as rapidly as possible, not at the convenience of the part-time student. Evening colleges are being diverted from the part-time students in order to provide facilities for the day students. We need scholars, teachers, and scientists, whether it takes four years to prepare them, or ten. The individual must not be discriminated against because he is a part-time student. As a person he has the same right to higher education as the full-time student. Only after pressure from AUEC and other groups has the part-time student been recognized as eligible for federal aid.

Diekhoff, John S. *The Future of Cleveland College*. Center for the Study of Liberal Education for Adults, Chicago, 1960. 49 pp.

In a memorandum for the guidance of a planning committee considering the future of Cleveland College, the adult education division of Western Reserve University, Diekhoff describes the Cleveland College programs and considers likely trends and problems for the future. Populations served, curriculum, problems of enrollment projections, financial policies, and a wide range of other topics are discussed as they relate to the credit and noncredit work of Cleveland College. Though considered in a particular context, the matters examined are of common interest in evening colleges.

Drazek, Stanley J., and others, eds. *Expanding Horizons . . . Continuing Education; The Golden Anniversary Publication of the NUEA*. National University Extension Association, Minneapolis. North Washington Press, Wash., 1965. 271 pp.

A golden anniversary commemorative publication. History of NUEA. Brief institutional reports of charter members and of institutions which have joined since 1915. Lists of annual conference locations, past presidents and secretaries of the Association. List of divisions and committees.

Dryer, Bernard V. "Lifetime Learning for Physicians; Principles, Practices, Proposals." *Journal of Medical Education*, June 1962.

A review of the present state of continuing education in medicine and a proposal for a "university without walls" for drastic improvement through a nation-wide cooperative program. Basic assumptions: continuing education of physicians is one of the most important problems facing medical education; there is a serious gap between knowledge and application in medical practice; continuing medical education is a national problem requiring a national plan for solution. Criteria for successful continuing education programs for physicians: direct and personal meaningfulness to the individual; complete freedom to participate or not; easy accessibility; continuity; utmost convenience. A national plan incorporating these features is suggested, with extensive exploration of the possible use of new methods and media and of the production of teaching materials.

Dyer, John P. *Ivory Towers in the Market Place; The Evening College in American Education*. Bobbs-Merrill, New York, 1956. 205 pp.

Though now out-of-date in some respects, this volume is still a useful introduction to evening college education. Written in a style which makes it very accessible to the general public, it reviews the need for evening education, types of persons typically involved, types of programs, problems of faculty and organization, etc. Extensive bibliography.

Ellwood, Caroline. *Survey of University Adult Education in the Metropolitan Area of New York*. New York University, School of Continuing Education. Fund for the Advancement of Education, New York, 1967. 166 pp. ED 013 405

This survey of university-level adult credit and noncredit courses covers over 30 colleges and universities in greater New York—largely evening colleges, community colleges, and community service programs. A historical review portrays the growth of liberal adult education since the founding of Cooper Union in 1859. A survey of adult educators showed largely nonprofessional part-time instructors of diverse backgrounds and a need for more in-service training and closer communication with administrators and other faculty. Recommendations include: a Center for Continuing Education in New York, coordinated self-study by all university adult education divisions, joint planning to determine future areas of concern, seminars for community leaders, continuing education on urban problems, and special programs to upgrade the education and social awareness of disadvantaged adults. Also noted are 15 programs primarily for women, 20 projects in New York State under Title I of the Higher Education Act of 1965, and six special degree programs. The document includes numerous charts and tables and 33 institutional profiles.

English, J. M. "Some Economic Questions Concerning Lifelong Learning." In *The New Challenge in Lifelong Learning*, pp. 33–37. University of California, Los Angeles; University-wide Academic Senate Committee on University Extension, 1965.

Discusses the relationship between alternative policies of investment for development and financial responsibility in California university extension programs and how the ultimate social and financial benefits to California citizens and taxpayers can be assessed in determining financial policies in extension.

Erickson, Clifford G., and others. *Eight Years of TV College; A Fourth Report*. Chicago Board of Education, 1964. 40 pp.

Summary report of experience with eight years of the Chicago TV College program of junior college credit courses by television. The program was extremely successful. Data are presented and problems outlined on curriculum offered; achievement and retention of learning; types of faculty and special training for TV presentations; costs; types of students enrolled and retained; relationships of the TV college to the regular junior college programs; and expectations for the future.

Farmer, Marth L., ed. *Student Personnel Services for Adults in Higher Education*. 1967. 210 pp. AC 001 451

This reference work on personnel services in evening colleges includes papers on the historical background of evening colleges and on student personnel services; administrative organization; admissions; student activities; counseling; placement; training of personnel workers; service to business, industry, and labor; financial aid; and the implications of automation and cybernation for evening education and for the personnel and guidance profession. The impact of adult motivation and circumstances, distinctions between personal or psychological counseling and other forms of counseling and guidance, professional and personal requisites for student personnel workers, the planning of adult-centered extracurricular activities, and the problem of access by part-time students to private loans, veterans' benefits, and federal loans and grants under the revised National Defense Education Act and the Higher Education Act of 1965, are stressed. The document includes a subject index. This document is available from the Scarecrow Press, Inc., Metuchen, N.J.

Flaugher, Ronald L., and others. *Credits by Examination for College Level Studies, an Annotated Bibliography.* Educational Testing Service, Princeton, N.J., 1967. 230 pp. AC 002 179

This annotated bibliography contains 308 items on transfer students and transfer policy, student accreditation by examination, and sources of instruction for unaffiliated students. The first section features descriptions of policies, problems, and recommendations concerning transfer students and research studies on their performance and characteristics. The section on accreditation by examination covers the role of the credit system in American higher education, arguments for and against credit by examination, student performance and characteristics, the College Entrance Examination Board Advanced Placement Program, large scale institutional programs (Brooklyn College, University of Buffalo, New York Proficiency Examinations), and general policies and practices. The last section contains studies on correspondence study for college credit, college level courses by television, college extension services and adult education courses, and college credit for military experiences. Pre-1945 materials are grouped separately as being mainly of historical interest. The document includes an author index. It is available from the College Entrance Examination Board, Publications Order Office, Box 592, Princeton, N.J. 08540.

Ford Foundation. *Urban Extension; Report on Experimental Programs Assisted by The Ford Foundation.* 1966. 52 pp. ED 011 095

This report outlines the experiences of 8 universities and a nonacademic community development organization which had received Ford Foundation grants for urban extension programs. Each organization used the approach best suited to its size and structure, and the skills and talents of staff personnel. The most significant consequence of most of the experiments lay in helping local communities create structures for the war on poverty, enhancing the ability of universities to serve state and local governments in shaping community action programs to meet federal requirements, creating a working liaison between the universities and government agencies, and crystallizing several critical questions which universities must resolve to function effectively in urban affairs. The recipient universities were Wisconsin, Rutgers, Delaware, California at Berkeley, Missouri, Oklahoma, Purdue, and Illinois. The community organization was ACTION-Housing, Pittsburgh. Bibliography pp. 40–43.

Frandson, Philip E. *Higher Adult Education, Its Present and Future; Analysis and Projections Based on Six Years of Program and Registration Data, 1960–1966.* Joint AUEC-NUEA Committee on Data and Definitions, 1967. 19 pp. ED 014 648

This is the second time-span (1960–1966) description and analysis of program and registration data for member institutions of the Association of University Evening Colleges and the National University Extension Association. Among the reliability limitations of the data were fluctuations in the number of institutions reporting, questions as to the accuracy with which the data were classified in terms of program type and credit type, and the inability of certain institutions to provide all of the requested data. Because of the difficulty of assessing the relative importance of variables which account for the increase in programs, registrations, and students, it was necessary to compute adjusted percentage increases. Data are included on average number of programs and registrations, percentage increases in programs, credit type (degree, nondegree, and noncredit), form of courses (class, conference, and correspondence study), subject categories, and percentages of men among the class and correspondence students. Registrations in adult higher education during 1960–2000 in relation to population are projected. This document is also available from the Office of the Executive Secretary, Association of University Evening Colleges, University of Oklahoma, Norman, Okla. 73069.

Franklin, Richard, ed. *Patterns of Community Development.* 1966. 363 pp. AC 000 335

Case histories of systematic community development in southern Illinois involving eight rural communities (including all of Pope County) and East St. Louis provide examples of grass roots decision-making in social, cultural, commercial, industrial, educational, and civic betterment and illustrate basic approaches to community and regional development— educating youth, working with adult populations in attempting gradually to change habits and attitudes, and introducing outsiders to initiate change. Experiences relevant to the role of university planning consultants and to the training of community development personnel are considered. Questions, issues, and hypotheses are framed for future social actional research. Basic objectives of community development are briefly discussed. This document is available from the Public Affairs Press, 419 New Jersey Avenue, S.E., Washington, D.C. 20003.

Friedmann, Eugene A. "Changing Value Orientation in Adult Life." In *Sociological Backgrounds of Adult Education,* edited by Hobert W. Burns, pp. 39–64. 1964.

Value orientations are discussed in terms of major adult roles in our society; cyclical shifts influencing performance in specific roles; consequences of role loss; influences of value orientation on selection of new goals and role activities; and relationships between value orientation and socialization processes (education or preparation for living) during adulthood. Characteristics of vocational, avocational, and family careers are outlined. Shifting goals and adult education participation are discussed. The case history of a residential seminar is presented as an indication of increasing interest among older adults in liberal, nonvocational, leisure-oriented education.

Fund for Adult Education. *A Ten Year Report of the Fund for Adult Education, 1951–1961.* White Plains, N.Y., 1962. 127 pp.

Final ten-year report of the work of the Fund for Adult Education, briefly recounting its extensive work in educational television, the development of liberal education study-discussion programs and programs of education for public responsibility, fellowship programs, and general support of adult education organizations. Lists of grantees, projects, publications, and a financial accounting.

Glancy, Keith E. *Noncredit Adult Education at the University Level; A Summary Report.* Studies in Higher Education, number 88. Purdue Univ., Lafayette, Ind., Division of Educational Reference, 1958. 23 pp.

Summary report of author's 1958 thesis presents practices and attitudes regarding noncredit university adult education as shown in questionnaires from 524 academic administrators and teaching personnel in 293 colleges and universities with noncredit adult programs and by responses from 40 institutions without such programs. Patterns of sponsorship, provision of teaching staff, participants in program-planning, sources of funds, and types of clientele are outlined. Opinions on instructor qualifications, suitable scope and level of courses, cooperation with outside groups, clientele participation in program planning, and responsibility for financial support and program administration are cited. Major points of consistency or inconsistency between opinions and actual practices are noted, and differences in attitudes toward administrative and operational practices are briefly examined in relation to selected characteristics (sponsorship, location, size of community, enrollment, type of program, areas of responsibility, administrative staff, etc.). Appendix: 74-item opinion questionnaire. List of publications on higher education.

Glaser, William A., and Sills, David L. *The Government of Associations; Selections from the Behavioral Sciences.* 1966. 273 pp. AC 001 661

A compilation of 47 selections from books, journals, and research reports in the behavioral sciences, this book of readings either about voluntary associations or with implications for them is addressed to leaders, board members, working volunteers, and staff members of voluntary associations and to behavioral scientists and social workers interested specifically in voluntary associations. A representative selection of the research literature and a wide range of points of view are presented. An important difference between voluntary associations and business firms—that leadership in voluntary associations is to a much greater extent based upon the consent of the participants—is stressed. Since not enough research has been carried out exclusively on voluntary associations, some selections concern other private organizations, such as businesses, trade unions, and factories. Sections are: the social origins and types of voluntary associations; social influences upon the membership; the associations' influence upon society; voluntary associations in other societies (rural Japan and France); the nature and effects of leadership; and organizational structure, processes, communication, decision making, goals, means, and change. This document is available from the Bedminster Press, Inc., Vreeland Ave., Totowa, N.J. 07512.

Goldman, Freda H. *The Arts in Higher Adult Education; A Second Review of Programs.* Center for the Study of Liberal Education for Adults, Boston, 1966. 82 pp. ED 010 867

A general description of the arts in the contemporary university precedes descriptions of specific adult program prototypes. The current place of the arts outside the university includes recent trends in art institutions, government, business, foundations, arts councils, publications, and educational television. Issues and problems concerning the role of the arts in society are discussed in relation to the education of the adult audience.

————. *A Turning to Take Next; Alternative Goals in the Education of Women.* Notes and Essays on Education for Adults, number 47. Center for the Study of Liberal Education for Adults, Boston, 1965. 64 pp. ED 017 839

In view of the fact that much of the participation of women in continuing higher education reflects attempts, often made in vain, at self-fulfillment in the sphere of paid employment, educators ought to reassess the whole range and rationale of individuals and as members of society; strongly suggests that existing educational provisions are inadequate in both respects. Moreover, middle class working women may be the first large group displaced by automation, and with their economic roles being eliminated and their free time increasing, working women are now being confronted with many of the problems foreseen for the automated society of the future. However, alternative life styles, based on politics, voluntary service, learning and scholarship, and appreciation and support of the arts, could be evolved, and a radically new type of school or curriculum could be developed with the aim of preparing and reeducating women for their chosen leisure occupations.

————. *University Adult Education in the Arts; A Descriptive View of Programs.* CSLEA Reports. Center for the Study of Liberal Education for Adults, Chicago, 1961. 72 pp.

A review of changing climate in the arts, noting the greater activity of a range of community organizations. Discussion of the relative emphasis on the three major purposes of university adult education in the arts: training producers of art; developing appreciation and understanding; bringing art to the community through exhibits, recitals, etc. Examples of programs from various universities are discussed by art form, e.g., visual arts, music, writing, theater, etc. Gaps in programming and possible new directions are reviewed.

Gordon, Morton. *Daytime School for Adults; A New Program Dimension at University of California, Berkeley, with a Reaction by Virginia Bullard, Director of Daytime Programs for Adults, Northeastern University.* CSLEA Occasional Papers, number 15. Center for the Study of Liberal Education for Adults, Boston, 1967. 40 pp.

In 1964 the University of California Extension set up an autonomous Daytime Program which now offers 100 classes, conferences, and lecture programs in four locations in the San Francisco Bay area. How the daytime staff faced problems of academic credit, need for risk capital in an innovative effort, and management of faculty relations and its use of volunteers to reach into the community form the core of this report. Differences between the Daytime Program and the rest of University Extension are: new type of students are attracted, student and faculty energy is high, and faculty is easily recruited. In the future, increased enrollments, more emphasis on continuing professional education, and expanded programs for women are anticipated. Because of rising costs, the Daytime Program is seeking support from outside sources to augment student fees in financing top quality education. Virginia Bullard's insights on the issues of finance, credit, and audience involvement are based on her experiences with a similar program at Northeastern. The document includes tables and the questionnaire used to survey the need for the program. This document is also available from the Center for the Study of Liberal Education for Adults, 138 Mountfort St., Brookline, Mass.

Gould, Samuel B. "Comments on the NUEA Position Paper; A University Administration View of University Extension." In *Proceedings of the Annual Meeting of the National University Extension Association (46th, Santa Barbara, California, 1961)*, pp. 25–31.

Gould cites all-inclusive aims, marginal relationships to the university, inadequate financial policy, the stigma (deserved or undeserved) of inferior standards, and lack of faculty respect and support, as besetting weaknesses of university extension which can be inferred from NUEA position paper. Corrective steps are urged.

Gowin, D. B., and Daigneault, George H. *The Part-Time College Teacher*. CSLEA Research Report. Center for the Study of Liberal Education for Adults, Chicago, 1961. 63 pp.

Research report based on an extensive study by the author and his colleagues at the University of Bridgeport, focusing on the part-time teacher; suggests that many administrators are reluctant to expect the same performance from a part-time teacher as from a full-time faculty member. Presents two patterns of expectations: (1) the instructor is selected because he can teach at a specified time and for a small amount of money and be prepared for the job by a talk with the dean and a handbook, but no grasp of theoretical and philosophical aims of education is expected; (2) the potential teacher is given an educational program stressing theory and technique and is judged by professional standards. New ways of recruiting, selecting, and preparing part-time evening college teachers are discussed. Evidence is presented that a program of careful preparation will modify the ideas and attitudes which the prospective teacher holds about teaching.

Grimes, William, and deKieffer, Robert, eds. *The Status of Audiovisual Activities of NUEA Member Institutions*. National University Extension Association, Minneapolis, Division of Audiovisual Communications, 1962. 155 pp.

Results of a survey to determine the status of audiovisual activities and projected trends in institutions of the NUEA Division of Audiovisual Communications. Chapter 1: Background of the survey. Chapter 2: Institutional sponsorship and enrollment and the administrative relationships, lines of authority, and internal organization of audiovisual units. Chapter 3: Administrative details of staffing (positions, degrees held, academic rank, salaries, length of service, numbers employed) and budgeting (descriptions, percentages of institutional support, yearly or revolving budgets). Chapter 4: Distribution activities: type and scope of on-campus and off-campus film circulation, tape recording and filmstrip distribution systems, with related administrative problems. Chapter 5: Graphics services (brochures, charts, etc.), still photography, motion picture photography, and radio-television production, with information on phases of operation. Chapter 6: Teaching and utilization, including data on courses in audiovisual communications and state and educational requirements. Chapter 7: Historical background of audiovisual activities and responses concerning plans for growth and expansion. 71 illustrations. Appendices.

Grinager, Patricia. "Extension Education by Land-Grant Colleges and Universities through Television." Ph.D. dissertation, Stanford University, 1964. 401 pp.

Dissertation synthesizes materials on extension education by land-grant colleges and universities through television. The author used W. H. Cowley's "A Taxonomy for the Study of Social Institutions" as an aid in managing the objective. Sixteen of 68 land-grant institutions have either a whole- or part-time share in a structure broadcasting on open circuits to general audience adults. Official statements of policy as they appear in federal legislation, as well as formal declarations by philanthropic foundations and land-grant institutions, are reviewed. Current teaching and related research as they apply to students not confined in classrooms are described. Although original purposes emphasized the continuing education of adults, actual practices increasingly favor in-school populations of younger persons. Extension educational television personnel include both educators-who-broadcast and broadcasters-who-educate. Describes the clientele by age, educational level, minority group membership, residence, socioeconomic class, sex, and marital status. Traces the funds that got educational television off the ground, beginning with original foundation philanthropy, gradually tending toward cooperative tax support. Inventory of transmitting and receiving facilities. Surveys a wide variety of constitutional, institutional, and associational controls that undergird extension education by land-grant colleges and universities through television. Traces these controls from the days of radio-telegraphy and radio-telephony.

Hamilton, Thomas H. "Adult Education; Task of the University." In *Growing Time,* pp. 52–57. CSLEA Notes and Essays on Education for Adults, number 44. Center for the Study of Liberal Education for Adults, Boston, 1964.

The function of a university in both teaching and research (for students in residence as well as for adults) is to lead students and research apprentices from the specific, the concrete, and the particular to the general, the abstract, and the theoretical. The same criteria should be applied to adult programs as to regular programs, but they should be stated in terms of principles rather than mechanics.

Hattery, Carolyn P., and others. *A Midwest World Affairs Audience; Interest in World Affairs and its Origins.* University Extension Division, University of Wisconsin, Madison, 1959. 44 pp.

Reports on the characteristics of adults who participate in world affairs education courses. Conclusions are that well-established Jewish and "old-stock" Protestant Americans are most likely to take an active interest in the subject and their interest is initiated by a number of factors, most important of which seems to be an intellectually stimulating family life, and the least important, adult education activities or exposure to mass media. Their broad range of civic activities reflects a feeling of responsibility to be well-informed and this culminates in an interest in world affairs. Adult education appears to have two central tasks in the field of world affairs: to create an initial interest among those who do not recognize the importance of understanding international relations and to provide those who are already aware of the importance with opportunities to broaden and deepen their knowledge and insight.

Havighurst, Robert J. "Changing Status and Roles during the Adult Life Cycle; Significance for Adult Education." In *Sociological Backgrounds of Adult Education,* edited by Hobert W. Burns, pp. 17–38. 1964.

Discusses the relationship between instrumental education (preparation for future gain) and expressive education (education basically for its own sake) throughout adulthood. Typical roles and development tasks of the adult life cycle and concerns that dominate each decade are described. Extension of expressive or intrinsic forms of adult education, more effective services to adults over 50, and expanded service to working-class adults, are viewed as major tasks for the future.

Haygood, Kenneth. "Shaping the Urban Culture; The Role of Higher Education in the Evolving Urban Scene." In *Roles for the Evening College in the City of Tomorrow; Proceedings of the Annual Meeting of the Association of University Evening Colleges (24th, 1962)*, pp. 57–63.

The greatest challenge for university adult education is developing a better understanding of urbanization on the part of the individual citizen. The university is the social institution to provide intellectual leadership, and the evening college is in a strategic position to stimulate the university to assume this leadership. The peril in allowing our urban culture to develop haphazardly is an attendant lack of personal meaningfulness, allowing people to develop as benign, placid, and acquiescent citizens who do not challenge the growth of our culture.

————. *The University and Community Education.* CSLEA Notes and Essays on Education for Adults, number 37. Center for the Study of Liberal Education for Adults, Chicago, 1962. 64 pp.

Haygood examines types of community-oriented programs sponsored by academic institutions, discusses problems inherent in planning and executing programs, and comments on advantages and disadvantages of various approaches to community action and service. Scope, objectives, and requirements of community development are considered, and community service functions of universities are suggested.

Hendrickson, Andrew. "The Role of Universities in the Education of the Aged." *Adult Education,* spring 1962, pp. 162–64.

Responsibilities of universities for research on education of the aged are indicated, difficulties in determining and meeting educational needs of older people are noted, and a proposed study involving 2200 subjects 65 and over in Columbus, Ohio, is outlined.

Horn, Francis H. *Promoting High Standards of Professional Excellence.* CSLEA Occasional Paper, number 9. Center for the Study of Liberal Education for Adults, Boston, 1964. 13 pp.

Horn raised the issue of whether the traditional credit evening college should be entirely separate from the noncredit program or whether the two should be operated in the same unit. He recommends that evening colleges adopt a basic philosophy, organization, and program of their own, playing a unique role not shared with other colleges in the university. Their role should be seen, not just as duplicating educational services provided by the day colleges for adults whom circumstances have forced to complete their formal education on a part-time basis, but providing informal educational services, some with little or no relation to what the institution is doing in its day division. If evening colleges are to meet the challenge of the next 25 years for continuing education for adults, both excellence and standards must be measured in the light of the unique role and responsibility of the evening college.

————. "Tomorrow's Targets for University Adult Education." Address to tenth annual seminar on leadership in university adult education, Michigan State University, 1967. 15 pp. AC 000 610

Scientific and technological advances, the population explosion, increasing leisure, rising educational levels and expectations, and the growing complexity of public issues and other facets of modern life have direct implications for university adult education. Although the adult educational role of liberal arts colleges and junior colleges will, and must, continue to increase, universities must provide leadership in this area because they alone are committed to the improvement of society in all its aspects and have the personnel to contribute significantly to the task. Objectives must include not only doctoral and postdoctoral work and professional continuing education but also the expansion of liberal arts education in both the sciences and the humanities and provision for groups (notably women and retired persons) who have not been part of the regular clientele of university adult programs.

Houle, Cyril O., and others. *The Armed Services and Adult Education.* American Council on Education, Washington, D.C., 1947. 257 pp.

The purposes of this descriptive study conducted after World War II were: (1) to inventory all voluntary educational programs of the armed forces, (2) to provide a panoramic description of the programs, and (3) to indicate their major implications of practical value to civilian adult educators. The mass of information, including much statistical data, is organized by branch of service within chapters on history and purpose; personnel and organization; correspondence study; methods of individual and group instruction; "post-hostilities schools," i.e., off-duty, voluntary preparation for return to civilian life; programs of general orientation and information; library services; literacy training; guidance activities; methods of motivation and recruitment of participants; evaluation methods. Specific implications are listed in the following areas: adult education objectives, administration and organization, methods, instructional materials, leadership training, guidance and counseling, student recruitment, evaluation. Bibliography, list of sources and informants.

Houle, Cyril O. "Conditions for Leadership in the Total Program of Public Affairs in a State." Address to the Division of Agriculture, National Association of State Universities and Land-Grant Colleges, Washington, D.C., Nov. 14, 1966. U.S. Department of Agriculture, Division of Extension Research and Training, 1967. 12 pp. ED 012 861

A narrative about the president of West Dakota A & M University provides a discussion of the role of university extension in public affairs education. In this land-grant college, the extension service was only the largest of numerous adult programs on and off campus. Other institutions, using the Cooperative Extension Service as a model, were developing urban extension programs funded by Title I of the Higher Education Act. The president felt that off-campus programs should be coordinated under a vice-president, a state agency should be created to coordinate programs of universities and other agencies, and a commission created to allocate federal funds. Target audiences could be defined as specialists (teachers and administrators), the actively concerned (PTA members), the attentive (listeners), and the inattentive (apathetic). Objectives suggested by this framework were that specialists could educate each other, interested citizens could be provided with subject knowledge and techniques, leadership training could be provided for the attentive and motivation for the inattentive. The Cooperative Extension Service had much to offer in urban extension, in subject specialists and social expertise in leadership training, group dynamics, use of mass media, and locating and influencing leaders of the power structure.

————. "The Evening College." *Journal of Higher Education,* October 1954, pp. 362–73.

Describing the rise of an imaginary university and the shaping of its extension programs, Houle illustrates his conception of the evening college as an educational bridge between the academic community and the community at large.

————. "From Craft toward Profession." In *The Continuing Task; Reflection on Purpose in Higher Continuing Education.* Center for the Study of Liberal Education for Adults, Boston, 1967. 18 pp. AC 001 064

According to Houle, the early years of the Center for the Study of Liberal Education for Adults were a time for consolidation, setting of standards, and efforts aimed at more flexible, less vocationally oriented, more imaginative and relevant university extension programs. Despite frequent financial and other reverses, university extension has introduced such new services as adult degree programs, advanced management training, special programs for women, adult counseling, and urban extension work. Higher adult education in the professions and in industry has also flourished. However, largely because of these successes, leaders in higher adult education must struggle to keep their numerous administrative tasks from divorcing them completely from basic adult teaching and innovation. To accomplish this, the extension administrator must view his work, not as a craft based on customary activities and individual experience, but as a true profession guided by liberal values and theoretical analysis. Footnotes.

————. *Major Trends in Higher Adult Education.* CSLEA Notes and Essays on Education for Adults, number 24. Center for the Study of Liberal Education for Adults, Chicago, 1959. 47 pp.

A review of major trends in higher adult education, with brief consideration of a variety of policy problems in various types of higher education institutions. Contains a section on the coordination of agricultural and general extension and another on the rise of junior college adult education.

————. "The Obligation of the Junior College for Community Service." *Junior College Journal,* May 1960, pp. 502–16.

In the context of a mythical New Francisco Community College, Houle reviews some of the literature and current practices in junior college adult education, noting discrepancies between statement and practice. He examines the possible roles of the junior college, recommending: extending terminal education programs in occupational fields to adults already employed; a two-year curriculum especially for adults; more liberal, general, and cultural studies offered to the whole community; extension of guidance services to adults; collaboration with other adult education agencies; a broad program of courses, lectures, discussion groups, and other community-oriented offerings. Methods and problems of organization, administration, and curriculum development are briefly discussed.

Houle, Cyril O., and Nelson, Charles A. *The University, the Citizen, and World Affairs.* American Council on Education, Washington, D.C., 1956. 179 pp.

An effort, based on self-studies in 57 universities, interviews, and review of the literature, to define the unique role of the university in education for world affairs and the methods which seem most effective. Introductory chapters consider what citizens know and need to know about world affairs, their role in world affairs, and problems of identifying potential audiences. Subsequent chapters take up the following aspects of the subject: (1) description of university programs and the principles defining its role; (2) analysis of kinds of activities and their relation to the organizational structure of the university; (3) education suited to four groups of citizens: the inattentive, the attentive, the actively concerned, and the specialist; (4) proposed action program based on explicit goals for each audience. Note on method of the study. Bibliography.

Ingham, Roy J., ed. *Institutional Backgrounds of Adult Education; Dynamics of Change in the Modern University.* CSLEA Notes and Essays on Education for Adults, number 50. Center for the Study of Liberal Education for Adults, Boston, 1966. 115 pp.

Papers on various aspects of American higher education, with emphasis on the problems of effecting change in this institutional environment. R. J. Ingham, in an introduction, raises the question of how university adult educators can best use the information in these background papers which are not explicitly focused on adult education implications. John Corson examines the role of leadership and external forces in causing change, using six major changes as examples; Burton Clark uses Antioch, Reed, and Swarthmore to illustrate the concept of institutional "character"; Edmund Volkart explores the role of faculty and administration in institutional change; Howard Becker notes the importance of the particular perspectives of the students and the influence of student culture on attempts to institute change; Homer Babbidge maintains that all important changes have been evoked by forces outside the university community; Peter Blau examines universities as administrative structures, especially as they differ from other complex administrative units.

Iowa, University of, Iowa City; Institute of Public Affairs. *Community Development.* Proceedings of the Division of Community Development, 52nd annual meeting, National University Extension Association, April 22-25, 1967. 1967. 58 pp. ED 012 879

In papers presented at the 1967 meeting of the National University Extension Association, a university extension director; academic experts on community theory, regional and community affairs, and agricultural economics; and federal administrators discuss issues and ideas affecting the role of higher education in helping to improve communities. The requisites for purposive social change are examined against the backdrop of complex social structures and rapidly changing social relationships and values. A hierarchical geographic model is set forth to illustrate a conception of urban growth and functions. Community development is viewed in terms of the kinds of leadership needed to help citizens meet economic and other problems that require group decision and group action. A proposed college public-service training program would engage students (mainly university undergraduates) in seminars, workshops, and practical service to the community, either during the school term or in vacation periods. Finally, two assessments of the outlook for community service and planning policy under Title I of the Higher Education Act of 1965 give evidence of both success and failure in developing comprehensive, interdisciplinary programs founded on the basic processes of social change.

Jensen, Gale, ed., and others. *Adult Education; Outlines of an Emerging Field of University Study*. Adult Education Association of the U.S.A., Washington, D.C., 1964. 334 pp.

This book is concerned with the development of a more complete description of the field and body of knowledge of adult and continuing education required for graduate training programs for adult educators. The sixteen chapters, written by university professors of adult education, are in four sections: (1) a delineation and description of the milieu in which a graduate program for the training of adult educators is emerging; (2) adult education and other disciplines; (3) theories about determining objectives for adult education activities, programs and management of the learning situation; and (4) implications for programs of graduate study in adult education. The commission of the Professors of Adult Education is explained in an appendix.

Johnstone, John W. C. "Adult Uses of Education; Fact and Forecast." In *Sociological Backgrounds of Adult Education,* edited by Hobert W. Burns, pp. 89–128. 1964.

Results of an inventory by NORC of adult education activities in the United States during June 1961–May 1962 are summarized, with criteria for defining and categorizing such activities. Subject matter in formal adult education and in self-study, methods of formal study, and estimated attendance of variously sponsored courses are indicated. Participation is analyzed by age, sex, occupation, family income, size and type of community, family status, subject matter of first course, reasons for the most recent participation during the previous five years. General evaluations of course effectiveness suggest that courses are judged most effective as preparation for a new job or occupation. The potential audience for adult education is estimated at well over 30 million by 1982.

————. "Leisure and Education in Contemporary American Life." In *Perspective on Automation,* pp. 27–32. CSLEA Notes and Essays on Education for Adults, Number 43. 1964.

Discussion of social class patterns that have implications for adult education in an automated society. The most relevant social class differences in the perception and evaluation of education are: (1) lower classes place less emphasis on the importance of higher education; (2) the average deprived person is interested in education in terms of how useful it can be to him; (3) the lower-class person is less ready than his middle-class counterpart to engage in continuing education even in situations where tangible economic gains are offered as reward; (4) the typical lower-class person does not think of education in terms of personal growth or self-realization and is even less ready to turn to adult education for recreational purposes than for purposes of vocational advancement. For a sizeable sector of the population, continuing learning is understood and appreciated only in the language of tangible benefits, concrete rewards, and practical gains, and it is here that adult educators will face their most critical challenge in an age of automation.

Johnstone, John W., and Rivera, Ramon J. *Volunteers for Learning; A Study of the Educational Pursuits of American Adults.* National Opinion Research Center monographs in social research. National Opinion Research Center, Chicago, 1965. 624 pp. AC 000 461

Contemporary adult education in the United States today is examined by means of a national sample survey. In this monograph, adult learning is approached from a social psychological vantage point—the needs, motives, and satisfactions which impel adults to seek to learn some subject. The organization of adult education is considered only insofar as such organization facilitates or hinders individuals in the pursuit of learning. The extent and nature of adult participation in continuing education are reviewed; the people who engage in these pursuits are identified; the situations, circumstances, and personal goals which influence people to become involved in educational endeavors are reconstructed; the national climate of opinion regarding education for adults is looked at; and to a lesser degree, the range of facilities available for the instruction of the adult population is investigated. This document is available from Aldine Publishing Co., Chicago, Ill.

Joint AUEC-NUEA Committee on Data and Definitions. *Programs and Registrations, 1965–1966.* Norman, Okla., 1966. 22 pp.

Annual report of enrollment and registration data from AUEC-NUEA institutions. Data are presented by member institution, by types of program (classes, conferences, correspondence), and by broad subject categories. Summary tables by program type, by credit status, and by subject. List of definitions.

Joint AUEC-NUEA Committee on Minimum Data and Definitions. *Description and Analysis of Program and Enrollment Data, 1960–61 through 1962–63, and Projection of Future Enrollments.* Minneapolis, 1964. 28 pp.

Enrollment data for AUEC-NUEA institutions and analysis of trends in the period 1960–61 to 1962–63 with tentative projections into the future. Data by program types, e.g., classes, conferences, correspondence courses, discussion groups; by subject; by credit status, e.g., credit, noncredit, nondegree credit. Analysis of AUEC-NUEA differentiation. List of institutions; definitions of terms.

Kelley, R. L. "The Challenge of Self-Realization." In *The New Challenge in Lifelong Learning,* pp. 45–49. University of California, Los Angeles; University-wide Academic Senate Committee on University Extension; 1965.

The growing importance and magnitude of leisure in American society is described, and questions are raised concerning the role of extension education in fostering creative use of leisure.

Kellogg (W. K.) Foundation. *Continuing Education; An Evolving Form of Adult Education.* Battle Creek, Mich., 1960. 57 pp.

Recently developed programs and residential and conference facilities of the W. K. Kellogg Center at Michigan State University (opened 1951), the Georgia Center for Continuing Education at the University of Georgia (opened 1957), and centers at the Universities of Nebraska, Oklahoma, and Chicago are described and presented as distinctive contributions to the theory and practice of continuing education. Course content of conferences, workshops, and seminars; audiovisual equipment and services such as educational broadcasting and closed-circuit TV; participant characteristics; financial support and budgeting; provision for self-study and research; and special educational and public-service activities, are featured. Illustrations include photographs and floor plans of the centers.

Kidd, James Robbins. *Financing Continuing Education.* Scarecrow Press, New York, 1962. 209 pp.

The purposes of this book are: to collect and organize statements and data about financing continuing education; to consider experience from other fields of work and from other countries that may be relevant; to raise questions and present suggestions on financing continuing education. Common assumptions about financing adult education, including the notion that adults should pay its costs through tuition, are critically examined. Chapters on: typical financing patterns in various adult education institutions, sources of funds, role of governments, and the role of corporations. Other sources and financing patterns, some suggested by experience in other fields, are presented. Bibliography, index.

Klotsche, J. Martin. *The Urban University—and the Future of our Cities.* Harper and Row, Publishers, Inc., New York, 1966. 149 pp. AC 000 172

Urban universities now enroll nearly one-half of the students in degree-granting institutions. Because of this increasing trend, these urban universities are becoming an integral part of their respective communities. The major portion of the volume discusses aspects of the school-community relationship: (1) a profile of the urban university, (2) the role of the university with respect to its community, (3) the urban needs and the university resources which can fulfill these needs, (4) the urban campus and the difficulties it faces in expansion attempts, (5) the urban university student and the trend toward commuting, and (6) the urban university and mass exposure to the arts. The final chapter presents the problems which an urban culture imposes on an urban university and the responses necessary for coping with them successfully. This document is available from the publisher.

Knowles, Malcolm S. *The Adult Education Movement in the United States.*
Holt, Rinehart and Winston, New York, 1962. 335 pp.

This is the standard history of adult education in the United States, with
the evolution of university adult education and agricultural extension
traced in context of the whole field of adult education. Part II deals with
the development of coordinating organizations within segments of the field
and with the problem of developing a unifying national organization.
Section III discusses the nature and dynamics of the field of adult education
and reviews likely future developments. Extensive bibliography.

Knowles, Malcolm S., ed. *Handbook of Adult Education in the United States.*
1960. 631 pp. AC 002 199

Within this handbook are sections on the background, functions, and role
of adult education in American society; broad areas of concern in educational policy and planning (including the training of adult educators); the
institutional programs and resources of public, private, professional, and
voluntary organizations; major program areas (largely in the categories of
academic, vocational, and general education); and present trends and
future strategies in adult education. The document also includes an index,
chapter references, and a directory of national agencies, organizations, and
associations in adult education. It is available from the Adult Education
Association of the U.S.A., 1225 19th Street, N.W., Washington, D.C.
20036.

Knowles, Malcolm S. "Strategy for the Future." In *Growing Time,* pp. 63–68.
CSLEA Notes and Essays on Education for Adults, number 44. 1964.

Since most individuals will have to adjust to more than one cultural
revolution during a lifetime, the purpose of education must change. It is
no longer sufficient to transmit culture; instead, the individual must develop
the ability to discover knowledge or conduct inquiry. The learner must be
exposed at each stage of his growth to the issues, conflicts, contradictions,
tensions, and changes in his society. Primary concerns of formal schooling
should be: (1) has the individual developed an insatiable thirst for learning? (2) has he mastered the tools of inquiry? (3) can he read with
retention and comprehension? (4) does he have a fairly concrete but flexible plan for continuing learning? Until the schools are producing human
beings ready to engage in adult education, adult education has to remedy
the inadequacies of traditional youth education: it has to teach people how
to learn. Adult educators should lead in reorganizing knowledge and
developing a curriculum to provide for lifelong learning by adults who are
able to engage in inquiry. Thus, the adult educator will become the
professional leader in the total field of education, with continuing education
starting at birth and going on throughout life.

Knox, Alan B. *The Audience for Liberal Adult Education.* CSLEA Reports.
Center for the Study of Liberal Education for Adults, Boston, 1962. 47 pp.
AC 001 042

Clientele of specific liberal adult education programs (Great Books, UCLA,
University of Wisconsin, University of Chicago, Whittier College, New
York University, Syracuse University, Ways of Mankind, and the Laboratory College for Adults) are analyzed by age, adult roles, socioeconomic
level, education, and reasons for attending. Generalizations on patterns of

attendance are formulated, followed by evidence tending to support each generalization. Implications for planning and promotion of programs both for the general audience (typically middle-class and middle-aged) and for specific target audiences are discussed, and topics are suggested for research.

―――. *Research Arrangements within University Adult Education Divisions.* CSLEA Reports. Center for the Study of Liberal Education for Adults, Chicago, 1963. 38 pp.

Report of study concerning institutional arrangements for encouraging adult education research. Adult education research was most frequently found in larger universities, in adult education divisions characterized by large enrollments, several geographical locations, diversified subject matter offerings, a variety of education formats, and substantial influence on institutional policies regarding adult education. However, research arrangements can be established within any adult division, and much depends upon interest and commitment of staff members. Annual research expenditures ranged from less than $500 to more than $50,000, with average expenditures for divisions with internal financing about $1000, while those with outside financing average about $16,000. Most frequent shortcoming in research arrangements was lack of money to provide time and personnel, while the most frequent benefit cited was the contribution research findings made to program planning.

Kravitz, Sanford L. "Urban Institutions as University Clients." In *Political Backgrounds of Adult Education,* edited by Thomas Cummings, Jr. Center for the Study of Liberal Education for Adults, Boston, 1967. 13 pp. ED 011 363

The author discusses the ways in which the university can and must help the city solve its problems. He sees the two major needs of urban institutions as a manpower shortage and a knowledge problem. The university must mobilize its resources rapidly and responsibly not only to increase the number of workers available but to improve the quality and efficiency of these people. It must redefine job content, training, roles, and job status; reevaluate current notions about professionalism; and give attention to the increasing use of subprofessionals. In regard to the knowledge problem, the university must emphasize the application of knowledge to the improvement of society and work toward creative innovation, seeking new ways to relate its resources to community needs. It must also seek a common language to bridge the gap between the administrator's concern for immediate answers to specific problems and the scholar's concern for theory and research.

Leagans, Paul J. *Projections of Extension-Adult Education into the Next Decade (A Synthesis of Ideas Collected in Twelve Universities through a Semi-Structured Study).* Cornell University, Ithaca, N.Y., College of Agriculture, Division of Extension-Adult Education, 1966. 22 pp.

The main purpose of the study was to explore projections in thought and in action related to the form, role, and requisites of extension education during the next decade. The study consisted of individual and group interviews with administrators and professional colleagues in 12 universities widely dispersed over the U.S. The questions were related to the most likely form of the extension agency in the future—the kinds of competencies viewed as essential to effectiveness of an extension staff; the nature, need for, and content of graduate study in extension education; criteria useful in delineating in-service and graduate training programs; ways to provide needed training for international students; the nature of research expected of graduate students majoring in Extension-Adult Education. The responses were examined and presented in the following items: general pattern of thinking, form of the extension agency, trends in specifics, a profile, some projections.

Liveright, A. A. "Adult Education in Colleges and Universities." In *Adult Education in Colleges and Universities,* pp. 1–23. CSLEA Notes and Essays on Education for Adults, number 30. 1960.

Describes types of institutional arrangements for adult education in colleges and universities and summarizes data concerning clientele. Included is an outline of the rise of university adult education in the United States; socio-economic and educational factors influencing growth; vocational, intellectual, and cultural objectives of adult education; patterns of growth and organization; faculty resources and relationships; financial support; types of facilities; trends in program planning and instruction; and problems of support, sponsorship, and purpose confronting the university adult education movement.

Liveright, A. A., and Miller, Harry L. *Adult Education in Colleges and Universities; Liberal Adult Education.* CSLEA Notes and Essays on Education for Adults, Number 30. Center for the Study of Liberal Education for Adults, Chicago, 1960. 54 pp.

Two chapters reprinted from the *Handbook of Adult Education.* A. A. Liveright presents an overview of university adult education, its institutional arrangements, clientele, problems, and trends. Harry Miller reviews liberal adult education programs based on three model types: discipline oriented, liberating skill based, and education through liberating experiences.

Liveright, A. A., ed. *The Concept of Lifelong Integrated Learning, "Education Permanente," and Some Implications for University Adult Education.* International Congress of University Adult Education Occasional Paper, number 2 (New York University, August 5–7, 1967). International Congress of University Adult Education, 1968. 69 pp. ED 016 988

Working papers, presentations, and discussions at the 1967 seminar on "Education Permanente" convened by the International Congress of University Adult Education included UNESCO background material on the concept of lifelong integrated learning; the need and the prospects for greater flexibility and outreach at the university level; analyses of the economic, technological, sociological, and psychological dimensions of continuing education for contemporary world society; and case studies of professional and worker education in France. Emphasis in the presentations was generally placed more on understanding and insights, on appreciation and attitudes, than on facts and information alone, and on the need to minimize differences between teacher and student roles and between youth and adults. There was general agreement that universities, while stressing the assessment of values, should examine the wider society, develop "cultured" persons, inject liberal education into professional training, champion controversy, stimulate the full development of individual intellectual capacities, and serve as the nerve center for an extended system of social and intellectual communication. (Reactions from four other participants were also obtained.) Also noted were blocks and impediments to educational change, implications for the future of university adult education, and basic questions for further exploration.

Liveright, A. A. *National Trends in Higher Adult Education.* CSLEA Occasional Papers, number 2. Center for the Study of Liberal Education for Adults, Chicago, 1960. 10 pp.

Report on some of the trends appearing in the field of higher adult education: (1) basic reexamination of the field, as indicated by NUEA's analysis of the goals of general extension divisions, and by numerous other studies; (2) concern with financing of the field; (3) growth of credit activity and programming and building the idea of continuing education into the undergraduate division; (4) informal and noncredit programming for special audiences induced to participate through membership in institutions or organizations; (5) educational programs which build sequential studies and learning in depth; (6) steps to relate credit and noncredit offerings, such as the new special degree programs; (7) increasing interest in arts and cultural programs.

Liveright, A. A., and DeCrow, Roger. *New Directions in Degree Programs Especially for Adults.* Center for the Study of Liberal Education for Adults, Chicago, 1963. 38 pp.

Review of development of degree programs especially designed for adult, part-time students and the social needs which underlie this movement. Lists of characteristics common to the programs and the conditions which appear to be necessary for their success. Descriptions of the programs at Brooklyn College, Syracuse University, University of Oklahoma, Queens College, Goddard College, Johns Hopkins University, San Francisco Theological Seminary. Bibliography.

Liveright, A. A., and Goldman, Freda H. *Significant Developments in Continuing Higher Education.* CSLEA Occasional Papers. Center for the Study of Liberal Education for Adults, Boston, 1965. 28 pp.

New developments in higher adult and continuing education grouped into three categories: *A.* New climate and milieu: (1) the scope of adult education is broadening; (2) adult education is accepted as part of the educational design; (3) the federal government is active on its behalf; (4) local planning and cooperation are encouraged; (5) interest is increasing among professionals, leaders of industry, and publishers; (6) the "ivory tower" posture is no longer tenable; (7) universities are increasing their involvement in international aspects. *B.* Institutional changes include: (1) regional associations are becoming more active; (2) states are moving toward coordination and central planning; (3) possibilities of combining cooperative and general extension are receiving attention; (4) junior colleges are increasingly active; (5) many new national studies on adult education roles are under way. *C.* New program developments are: (1) degree programs for adults; (2) programs especially for women; (3) cultural programs; (4) urban education programs; (5) multi-media approaches; (6) independent study programs; (7) counseling for adults; (8) attention to continuity in education. Needs of the field can be grouped into three classes: (1) helping educators plan effective programs along the lines made possible by new appropriations, and providing for more opportunities in personnel training and professional development; (2) opportunity to try out ideas and develop new program models as demonstrations of what can be done; (3) need to evaluate and nurture new program directions.

Liveright, A. A. *A Study of Adult Education in the United States.* CSLEA Research Reports. Center for the Study of Liberal Education for Adults, Brookline, Mass., 1968. 147 pp. AC 002 699

Based on information gathered in 1965 and 1966 for the United States Office of Education, this study of adult education in the United States begins with a definition of terms and of underlying educational philosophy, then reviews the history of American adult education, current patterns of participation, the adult education profession (including research and the training of adult educators), the nature and scope of federal activities and policies, the present state of adult education activities by the mass media and other nonfederal groups and institutions, and areas of concern in the changing field of adult education. Recommendations for action are set forth in such areas as data reporting, research design, information dissemination, innovation and experimentation, interagency cooperation and program coordination within the federal government, and the recruitment, development, and training of qualified personnel. The document includes tables and chapter references.

————. "A Summary of Problems and Directions." In *Reorientation in Labor Education; A Symposium on Liberal Education for Labor in the University,* edited by Freda H. Goldman, pp. 111–17. CSLEA Reports.

A summary focusing on university liberal education for labor. Common problems are: (1) winning support, (2) providing for university-union cooperation, (3) adapting programs to a union audience. Recommendations are: (1) labor education experts in unions and universities must convince their institutions of the importance of programs for union members; (2) both unions and universities must face the problem of financing and must cooperate in supporting legislation for liberal adult education; (3) universities have a unique contribution to make in planning and offering broad, general, liberal education programs; (4) union-university policy committees must be extended so that differences, suspicions, and gaps in thinking may be overcome; (5) universities must improve the quality of teaching in programs for union members; (6) universities must overcome their reluctance to offer programs directed to union members.

————. *The Uncommon College; The College of Continuing Education at Metropolis University.* 1966. 28 pp. AC 000 626

Here is described hypothetical Metropolis University of 1980 with an undergraduate curriculum designed to provide a climate for lifelong learning and with a College of Continuing Education developed along lines of the four primary roles of adults: worker, family member, citizen, and self-realizing individual. Four Institutes serve the four roles. In addition three centers cut across the four Institutes to provide services and research to all of them—centers for counseling and community referral, for research and professional development, and for metropolitan studies and problem solving. Administrative and organizational arrangement involves a readily accessible campus for adults with a learning center, a small residential unit, and a museum for popular science. Faculty is obtained by a lend-lease arrangement with industry and government in Metropolis and use of faculty aides. Financing is diversified. Community cooperation is strong. New educational technology is exploited. The mythical quality of the University is belied by its roots in realities of the 1960s listed in the appendix.

Lockwood, Anne, ed. *Cumulative Indexes: Association of University Evening Colleges, Proceedings, 1948–58; National University Extension Association, Proceedings, 1915–57.* Center for the Study of Liberal Education for Adults, Chicago, 1960. 50 pp.

Combined author-subject indexes are cumulated for AUEC Proceedings and NUEA Proceedings. List of CSLEA publications.

Lowe, John. "Impressions of Adult Education in the United States." *Adult Education,* spring 1962, pp. 183–89.

A British observer compares the American and the British definitions and conceptions of adult education, comments on the work of the Adult Education Association and the Center for the Study of Liberal Education for Adults, discusses the predominance of vocational training and the tendency toward commercialism in American adult education, and suggests approaches to planning and research.

Lynch, Patrick, and Blackstone, Peggy L., eds. *Institutional Roles for In-Service Education of School Administrators. Task Force Seminar on Continuing Education of School Administrators of the University Council for Educational Administration (Albuquerque, New Mexico, April 27–30, 1966).* 145 pp. AC 001 862

A report of a task force seminar of the University Council for Educational Administration reviews the status and problems of in-service and continuing education of school administrators. Various authors consider the institutional arrangements for such education, the process of change in school systems, and new models for provision of in-service training of administrators. Papers are presented on continuing education in medicine and on management education programs. The role of the university and its relations with the school systems are considered. Included are implications and comments by seminar participants. There is a list of participants. The document is available from the University Council for Educational Administration, 65 South Oval Drive, Columbus, Ohio 42100.

Macy, John W., Jr. "The Newest Campus—The Federal Civil Service." In *Proceedings of the Annual Meeting of the National University Extension Association (49th, 1964),* pp. 45–49.

Highlights the educational needs of federal employees facing increasingly varied and complex managerial tasks and suggests means whereby universities can effectively contribute to their continuing career development.

Martin, Doris E. "The Role of the University in State Change; Perceptions of the Public Service Function in the Pacific West Coast Region. Summary of thesis. Teachers College, Columbia University, New York, 1963. 56 pp. AC 001 044

To explore the theoretical role and responsibility deemed proper for a state university concerning problems in the state resulting from rapid technological and cultural changes, university general extension administrators and other campus deans and administrators of the Universities of California, Hawaii, Oregon, and Washington and status leaders in those states were interviewed. Fifty-five interviews were held in all. The problem areas identified for respondents at the beginning of each interview were unemployment, urbanization, family dissolution, juvenile delinquency, mental health, aging, and problems of the state economy.

Matre, Richard A. "A Plea for the Practitioner." In *Counseling and Guidance in the Evening College; Proceedings of the Annual Meeting of the Association of University Evening Colleges (23rd, 1961)*, pp. 3–9.

Discusses the special function of AUEC as a meeting ground for evening-college administrators from diverse institutions with widely varying policies and advises moderation and impartiality in AUEC policy on credit and noncredit programs.

————. "Shaping the Urban Culture; A Viewpoint." In *The Roles for the Evening College in the City of Tomorrow; Proceedings of the Annual Meeting of the Association of University Evening Colleges (24, 1962)*, pp. 70–72.

The evening college role in higher adult education should be: (1) give adults the opportunity to learn what they should have learned earlier, (2) provide opportunity for lifelong learning, and (3) implant the desire to improve directly the conditions of life of man and his society. Shaping the urban culture is not the sole responsibility of the university, nor of the evening college. Government, church, voluntary organizations, elementary and secondary schools must join in meeting the conditions of evolving urbanization, and it would be the height of idiocy for every evening college to attempt to involve itself in a major way in the direct solution of the problems of urbanization. Before the evening college can do much about society, or groups within society, it must concern itself with the individual and his educational needs.

Matre, Richard A., and others. *A Live Option; The Future of the Evening College.* CSLEA Notes and Essays on Education for Adults, number 46. Center for the Study of Liberal Education for Adults, Boston, 1965. 97 pp.

Report of a study committee on the future of the evening college. Essays by Richard Matre, Ernest McMahon, George Daigneault, H. Lichtenstein, and Milton Stern take up such issues as separate administrative unit for evening work versus total university responsibility, confusions caused by handling credit and noncredit programs in one division, need for dramatic emphasis on creative programs which break with evening college academic traditions, tension between commitment to the university and commitment to community needs, the likely social milieu of the future, and the need to invent new evening college adjustments.

McConnell, Thomas R. "A Look at the Total Education Scene." In *The Changing University; A Report on the Seventh Annual Leadership Conference,* edited by George H. Daigneault, pp. 25–53. Center for the Study of Liberal Education for Adults, Chicago, 1959.

Discusses ways of promoting excellence in all segments of American society through different kinds and levels of institutions offering numerous kinds and levels of higher education. Questions are raised as to the future role of university adult education in the overall scheme of higher education.

McGhee, Paul A. "Three Dimensions of Adult Education." *The Educational Record*, April 1954, pp. 119–130.

An attempt to define three areas of adult education toward which higher education must formulate some policy. The first is the adult education movement with its role of "handmaiden of community action programs." Its spokesmen suggest that: (1) the truly important problems of adult education today are those which take place in community action groups, but colleges essentially stand apart from thousands of communities; (2) university commitment is to subject-matter scholarship, but the need of adult education is not for information but for experience in group work; and (3) universities have only teachers whereas the adult education movement needs group leaders. The second area is defined as the degree-credit school, with three problems identified: (1) the question of independence which the evening college will not have until it is recognized by the university as a college in its own right with a discrete function; (2) determination of purposes appropriate in terms of general university assumptions; and (3) the relationship of the evening college to the adult education movement, preferably no connection at all. The third area for policy decision includes noncredit, nondegree programs, semester-length or short courses, institutes, conferences, or any other kind of educational undertaking specially organized in response to the needs and interests of the community. These may well be the most useful, the most popular, and, in many cases, the most advanced work offered.

McGrath, Earl J. "Research on Higher Education for Adults." In *The Next Twenty-five Years; Proceedings of the Annual Meeting of the Association of University Evening Colleges* (25th, 1963), pp. 58–73.

Research is needed on the adequacy of programs for adults, including an analysis of the various programs which have been imaginatively designed, but not tried in practice, or have been tried and discontinued. Research is needed on the interests of persons who constitute the natural constituencies for part-time, off-hour instruction, including those who have never attempted to continue learning beyond their formal schooling, especially college graduates who ought to have established an interest in further self-enlargement. Related work could survey the relationships between the character and content of earlier education and the individual's motivation toward continuing education and the influence which earlier teachers have on continuing intellectual interests. Major premises which should characterize a suitable program for adults are: (1) the administrative unit and the teaching staff should have some identity of its own; (2) the mechanics of adult bookkeeping must be altered to fit adult students; (3) full advantage must be taken of devices and opportunities for self-education; (4) greater emphasis must be placed on evaluation of learning acquired through a wide variety of experiences other than classroom sessions; (5) the administration and trustees of institutions of higher education must value these adult programs on a par with all the other pressing educational needs of American society.

FORSYTH LIBRARY
FORT HAYS KANSAS STATE COLLEGE

McMahon, Ernest E. "Appropriate Curriculum." In *The Future and Uniqueness of Evening College Programs; Proceedings of the Annual Meeting of the Association of University Evening Colleges (22nd, 1960)*, pp. 27–36.

Appropriate determinants for a curriculum in university adult education are educational purpose, educational standards, and the extent of man's body of knowledge. Curriculum is dynamic and undergoing continuous change; therefore, the key word is "appropriate." Educational purpose should seek to attain in some measure three classical objectives: the good life, the useful, and the love of learning. Purpose meets with standards at the point of selection of students. Standards are a realistic concern to the evening college, as the adult credit student is highly motivated and he wants no question raised about the quality of his degree. Four descriptive classifications of students are suggested: (1) fully qualified to earn a baccalaureate degree; (2) potentially qualified to earn a baccalaureate degree; (3) not qualified to earn credit toward a degree; (4) with qualifications not determined. Two possible criteria for departure from the institution's regular undergraduate program are level and content. The curriculum for adults need not be identical to that of undergraduates. Illustration of these points is from experiences at University College of Rutgers.

————. *The Emerging Evening College; a Study of Faculty Organization and Academic Control in Ten Eastern University Evening Colleges.* Teachers College, Columbia University, New York, 1960. 163 pp.

Drawing on his study of a number of evening colleges, McMahon discusses in depth many of the common problems of university evening colleges. Chapters deal with history and growth of the movement, the variety and changes in evening college goals, academic standards, institutional arrangements and the problem of status, faculty arrangements, a review of the problems, and a projection of the evening college of tomorrow. An appendix traces the evolution of a separate evening college faculty at Columbia University and at Rutgers and a movement in that direction at Brooklyn College. Selected readings.

McNeil, Donald R. "The Role of the State University in Public Service." In *The New Challenge in Lifelong Learning*, pp. 23–31. University of California, Los Angeles; University-wide Academic Senate Committee on University Extension. 1965.

Essay on state university extension education calls for broad experimentation in planning and bold innovation in service. Educational needs are outlined in terms of clientele groups (business, industry, agriculture, labor, government, the military, and occupational groups) and problems and issues within society. Prospects for expanding and improving extension education through greater faculty involvement and administrative support, realigned institutional structures, and increased use of local, state, and federal funds, are discussed.

————. "Toward Greatness." Address to tenth annual seminar on leadership in university adult education, Michigan State University, 1967. 10 pp. AC 000 612

University extension in the United States is moving toward greatness because of an academic revolution that embraces changing technology, acknowledgement that lifelong learning is a necessity, and a realization that the public is not sufficiently well informed. Moreover, state and local governments are tending more and more to enlist the aid of the universities in public service. In order to realize the promise of greatness, however, university extension divisions require changes in the level of self support and improved reward system for extension instructors and professors, better means of recruiting and training extension personnel, and the strengthening of such national organizations as the National University Extension Association.

——. "The University and Adult Education." *Adult Education,* vol. 9, no. 2 1963, pp. 80–85.
Guidelines for the commitment of universities to adult education are: (1) there must be programs geared to the social needs of the area and clientele they serve, which include employment training and retraining, urban problems, public affairs, refresher courses for the aged, the professionals, and the semi-professionals, and leisure education; (2) greater unity within the ranks of adult educators, with unity and integration with the traditional faculty, and a solution of the agricultural and general extension stalemate; (3) heavy stress on research and experimentation connected closely with social needs. The key to these three points is financial support from the university policy makers who hold the purse strings of adult education. Ability to pay should not be the sole criterion for the adult student, and if private donations and local and state tax support are not sufficient, federal aid should be the answer.

Mead, Margaret. "Continuing our Present System Isn't Enough." In *Today and Tomorrow; Three Essays on Adult Education in the Future,* pp. 34–38. CSLEA Notes and Essays on Education for Adults, number 34. 1961.
A redefinition of education seems to be necessary, with some new distinctions, e.g., between the kind of education that is related to phases of maturation and the kind that is related to bodies of knowledge and skill. We need to examine our present attitude toward education throughout the life span with all its compartmentalization and segmentation in terms of subject matter and chronological age. Mead suggests continuing flow of learning and teaching consistent with maturational levels and interests rather than credits used as building blocks for certification.

Michigan State University, East Lansing, Kellogg Center for Continuing Education. *Proceedings of the Annual Seminar on Leadership in Continuing Education (11th, Kellogg Center for Continuing Education, Michigan State University, April 8–11, 1968).* 55 pp. AC 002 612
Proceedings of this April 1968 seminar at the Kellogg Center for Continuing Education, Michigan State University, underline the conviction that the final decades of the twentieth century will make almost impossible demands on the wisdom, skill, and vision of educators and leaders in continuing education. Seminar papers discuss potential socioeconomic trends and influences in America, the problem of assessing the basic nature of contemporary change, the challenge of renewing and rejuvenating democratic institutions, issues of consequence (inequality, the nature of education, the role of university extension, and others) in society and in continuing education, and the ultimate goals of education in the twenty-first century. Two special presentations describe the Oakland Plan (Oakland University,

Rochester, Michigan) for alumni education and elements of an inter-institutional educational project launched by the Negro College Committee on Adult Education.

Miller, Paul A. "The University and Adult Education." (Title supplied). Excerpts from an address presented at a conference on extension activities, University of Rhode Island, Kingston, Oct. 25, 1966. New England Center for Continuing Education, Durham, N.H., occasional papers, number 1. 1966. 8 pp. ED 011 618

Two forces are colliding in the life of the American university today— historic sentiment, nurtured by the faculty, and the pressure of public affairs which administrators have had to accommodate. Adult education is at the point of impact, and the basic questions about the role of the university necessary to meet the issue have not been raised. One of the most exciting ideas in higher education is the consortium. The regional center being developed in New England could become a model laboratory for a regional faculty of adult education which would relate institutions, conduct basic research, prepare graduate students, and teach adults. Title I of the Higher Education Act will be a source of funds but careful planning is imperative. A comradeship between Cooperative Extension Service and General Extension would extend resources by melding their expertise in methodology and philosophy. Finally, the presidents and trustees of institutions must realize that continuing education of adults is as vital as the education of adolescents. This function must be part of the normal budget of the institution, much like research and teaching, not an expendable extra.

Morton, John R. *University Extension in the United States; A Study by the National University Extension Association, Made with the Assistance of a Grant from the Fund for Adult Education.* University of Alabama Press, Birmingham, 1953. 144 pp. AC 001 866

A description of university extension services offered by National University Extension Association (NUEA) member institutions in 1951-52 is based on questionnaires submitted by 57 members of NUEA, conferences with university staffs of 35 NUEA members, and participation of staff from representative institutions in preparing this report. Chapters cover university extension history, objectives and functions, organizational structure, financing, facilities, faculty and staff, clientele and programs, and methods. There are a bibliography and 70 tables. The document was published by the University of Alabama Press, Birmingham.

National Institute of Labor Education, Washington, D.C. *Challenges to Labor Education in the 60's.* 1962. 93 pp.

Papers from a symposium in which various authors examine the impact of technology on a changing society, problems of urban life, labor leadership within the union and in society, the specifically educational challenges these trends imply, and a review of educational methods particularly effective in labor education. Commentary on the conference by William Abbott. A note on the National Institute of Labor Education.

National University Extension Association, Minneapolis, *Criteria and Standards.* University of Iowa, Iowa City, 1962. 12 pp.

NUEA correspondence study should be guided and evaluated by clearly stated criteria and standards which point to excellence and provide a way of measuring achievement. Standards are stated in the following areas: (1) philosophy; (2) instruction, i.e., academic quality, content, course design and methodology, evaluation, research and experimentation, credit recognition; (3) staff, including administrative and supervisory, instructional, special, and clerical; (4) student services, e.g., library facilities, audiovisual instructional materials, counseling service, and transcripts and certification; (5) administration, which includes type of organization, finance, management, public relations and records.

National University Extension Association, Minneapolis, Policy Statement Committee. "To These Tasks . . . ; The NUEA Position Paper." In *Proceedings of the Annual Meeting of the National University Extension Association (46th, Santa Barbara, Calif., 1961)*, pp. 18–25.

The position paper outlines what extension administrators believe to be the functions and necessary points of emphasis of the university today as it is concerned with university extension. The paper was prepared by H.R. Neville, Lorenz Adolfson, Julius Nolte, and Paul Sheats.

New York, State Univ. of, Albany. *The New York College Proficiency Examination Program.* New York State Education Department, Albany, 1967. 135 pp. ED 017 858

The New York State College Proficiency Examination Program (CPE) was established by the State Education Department to open up the state's educational opportunities to those who had acquired college-level knowledge in ways other than through regular classroom attendance. Faculty members of colleges and universities in New York state, working in committees, draw up examination specifications, write examination questions, rate candidates' answers to those questions, and determine levels of performance needed to acieve satisfactory CPE grades. The State Education Department itself does not grant course credit. This is left to the individual educational institution to do, or not to do, in a manner consistent with its standards. However, satisfactory performance on a CPE will be accepted by the State Education Department in lieu of specific course requirements for teacher certification. This document presents the background of the program, questions and answers about it, policy statements of New York colleges and universities regarding CPE, and a description of each examination including material covered and objectives tested. Special adult degree programs are listed.

——. *The Regents Tentative Statewide Plan for the Expansion and Development of Higher Education, 1964.* 1965. 168 pp. AC 002 120

The Regents Plan of 1964 is the first of a projected series of reports of higher education planning in New York State. The complex of higher education, including the over 200 publicly and privately controlled colleges and universities which are considered in statewide long-range planning, is described, followed by a discussion of the needs of higher education and the goals that must guide state planning if these needs are to be met. The long-range plans of State University and City University and the plans of privately controlled institutions are reviewed. A discussion of factors affecting costs and trends in expenditures and income concludes with an estimate of the total cost expected by 1970. There is a summary and perspective of the total Plan. Appendixes are lists of member institutions by region and county, reports relating to planning for higher education in New York State, selected information on New York State colleges and universities, Board of Regents policy statement on the comprehensive community college, residence and migration of college students in New York state (fall 1963), and special studies projected as a basis for future planning. There are 26 tables and 12 figures.

————. *The Societal Dimension; A Program of Continuing Education for the State University of New York.* Office of Continuing Education, 1967. 37 pp. ED 011 641

The New York State University master plan for continuing education calls for programs for those who have not achieved initial educational and occupational objectives and for those who have achieved initial educational objectives, for making its resources available for community service, for extending its cultural resources to the public, and for more fruitful cooperation with the contract colleges and private colleges and universities. Program elements will include conventional day and evening courses for part-time students, provisions for independent study (correspondence instruction, programed instruction, extensive use of audiovisual media, group study, telephone conferences, guidance and counseling, and use of library resources), residential continuing education centers, sequential and other noncredit courses for cultural enrichment and for updating skills and knowledge, and urban extension activities, e.g., leadership training and research and demonstration projects. The Central Administration Office of Continuing Education should be charged with statewide policy coordination and formulation, consultative services, and financial aid, with local campuses taking charge of basic planning and operation.

Nolte, Julius. "Finding New Strategies and New Approaches." In *Growing Time,* pp. 69-75. CSLEA Notes and Essays on Education for Adults, number 44. 1964.

Some propositions are related to administrative strategies in university adult education. They are: (1) provision for equality of educational opportunity, (2) acceleration of efforts to provide facilities to make equal education a reality, and (3) the urgency of our times emphasizing the need for adult education. General strategies suggested to improve adult education are: increased publicity aimed at persons with enough influence to form public opinion, support of extension legislation, support by university administrators in terms of budget. Specific strategies suggested include, variety of extension programs, superior personnel, use of new devices, and constant examination of activities to be sure they are meeting revealed needs.

Ohio Board of Regents. *Master Plan for State Policy in Higher Education.* Columbus, Ohio, Board of Regents, 1966. 170 pp.

Comprehensive report on higher education in Ohio and a master plan of priorities for developing the system. Cooperative extension is discussed on pages 119 and 120 which refer to a previous study of this area and a "critical" evaluation conducted by Battelle Memorial Institute. As a result of these studies, the objectives of cooperative extension have been redefined, area extension centers established, work more closely integrated in the College of Agriculture and many activities not clearly related have been curtailed. Continuing education is discussed on pages 120–22, largely a review of present programs and statement of needs prepared by a consultant. Recommendations suggest that the universities attend to the needs of professional continuing education and increase provision of short courses, workshops and other continuing education programs. Tables.

Ohio State Univ., Columbus. "Problems in Administering General University Extension Programs." Reports from a graduate student seminar in adult education at The Ohio State University, 1966. 1967. 106 pp. AC 000 491

The papers in this publication were written by graduate students of Ohio State in a seminar on Organization and Administration of Adult Education Programs with the overarching theme of Problems in Administering General University Extension Programs. The specific topics covered dealing with university extension programs are: policy guidelines, principles of organization, needed relationships, staffing, approaches, methods and techniques, financing, counseling, student personnel services, public relations, and evaluation in university extension.

Oklahoma, University of, Norman, Extension Division. *The University of Oklahoma's Adult Part-Time Students in the Years Ahead (1957–1970).* 1957. 47 pp.

Reports data on current trends in extension enrollments and extension use and attempts to predict future demands for these services in Oklahoma. Population trends for age distribution, level of education, occupation, and adult population of 23 largest cities were used as indicators of growth.

Pennsylvania State University, University Park. *General University Extension; A Report of a Symposium (University Park, Pa., 1959–60).* 1960. 100 pp. AC 001 859

Overviews on extension from eight universities—California, Colorado, Kansas, Louisiana, Michigan, Minnesota, Oklahoma, and Wisconsin—were presented by the deans or directors of the extension divisions at a series of two-day sessions conducted as a symposium for the continuing education staff at Pennsylvania State University. This publication summarizes the presentations and includes for each the history, institutional objectives and philosophy of extension, geographic settings, staff, programs, methods of operation, finances, relationships with other institutions and agencies, and expectations for the 1960s. Organization charts are shown for each institution, and an overview of Penn State's extension is appended.

Petersen, Renee, and Petersen, William. *University Adult Education; A Guide to Policy.* Harper and Brothers, New York, 1960. 308 pp. AC 001 846

Topics include general principles of adult education, educational policy (credit and noncredit courses, teaching methods and facilities, standards for degree programs, and community services), noneducational activities of universities, and university adult education in foreign affairs. Appendixes are cooperative extension and the land-grant system, and member institutions of NUEA and AUEC.

Pitkin, Royce S. *The Residential School in American Adult Education.* CSLEA Notes and Essays on Education for Adults, number 14. Center for Study of Liberal Education for Adults, Chicago, 1956. 51 pp.

Essays discuss the potential educational and psychological advantages of small residential adult schools to the American public. The accomplishments of the Danish folk schools and the achievements of similar programs in North America are cited. Appendix: descriptions of American and Canadian residential adult schools and programs.

Rosentreter, Frederick M. *The Boundaries of the Campus; A History of the University of Wisconsin Extension Division, 1885–1945*. University of Wisconsin Press, Madison, 1957. 210 pp.

A detailed history of the growth of the great pioneering university extension division with emphasis on the social context from which evolved the "Wisconsin idea" of extending the university to all the citizens of the state. Documents the ideas and actions of Van Hise, Lighty, Reber, and other extension pioneers and the growth of correspondence study, the Farmers Institutes, the School for Workers, and other aspects of Wisconsin Extension, many of them still in vigorous action today. Extensive bibliography. List of manuscripts consulted.

Roth, Robert M., ed. *A Conspectus to the Self-Study Project of University College, the University of Chicago*. CSLEA Reports. Center for the Study of Liberal Education for Adults, Chicago, 1964. 105 pp.

Part 1 of the synopsis of the 1958–59 self-study project of University College (now the Extension Division) outlines the history of adult education at the University of Chicago from 1892 to 1960. Part 2 reviews participant characteristics and strengths and weaknesses of the curriculum at the Downtown Center during the period 1958–60. Part 3 discusses numerous sociological characteristics of Downtown Center students, together with ACE aptitude-test standings and evening college achievement. The final chapter summarizes data on the composition, academic qualifications, opinions, attitudes, and practices of faculty who were teaching, or had recently been teaching, at the Downtown Center.

Rovetch, Warren. "Cooperative Extension and the Land-Grant System in University Adult Education." Appendix to *University Adult Education; A Guide to Policy*, by Renee Petersen and William Petersen, pp. 201–231. Harper and Brothers, New York, 1960.

The history and tradition of Cooperative Extension, its relationship to the university and to its nonuniversity sponsors, and the social changes which have brought to the fore its conflict of political sensitivity versus rigidity of organization and tradition are reviewed. A final section considers the problems of relating Cooperative and General Extension. Data are presented on the number of agents and sources of funds by state.

Schroeder, Wayne L., and Sapienza, Dunnovan L. "Public Junior College Adult Education Administrator." *Adult Education*, vol. 15, no. 4, pp. 241–6. 1965.

The typical public junior college adult education administrator of this study was a male 40–59 years old, was as likely to have been a teacher as a college administrator before his present position, had not recently been a graduate student, was hired from within or from schools of below college level, had at least a master's degree, and received his more advanced degree in either education or administration after 1949. These findings raise some significant questions, such as: (1) are graduate programs for junior college administrators and adult educators keeping up with personnel needs? (2) why aren't those majoring in adult education being hired as adult education administrators in junior colleges? (3) is below-college administrative experience adequate training for a person assuming the responsibilities of a junior college adult education administrator? (4) is teaching at any level adequate experiential background for the adult education administrator? (5) what is the relationship of job experience and previous education to the quantity and quality of adult education programs? (6) what is the relationship between the administrator's background and his attitude toward and cooperation with other adult education agencies of the community?

Serbein, Oscar N. *Educational Activities of Business.* American Council on Education, Washington, D. C., 1961. 180 pp.

Report of an extensive investigation of all aspects of the educational activities of American business and industry, both in programs operated by the companies themselves and in their out-of-company programs involving the formal school system at all levels. Chapters on the financial contributions of business to education, the administration of educational activities in business firms, analysis of the organization and case study examples of major in-company programs, out-of-company training programs, a case study of education in the IBM Corporation. A final chapter discusses problems of duplication, competition for resources and other aspects of the relationship of business educational activities to the formal educational system. Many tables of data on participation, curriculum, costs, and other aspects of the subject. Bibliography.

Shannon, Theodore J., and Schoenfeld, Clarence A. *University Extension (the Library of Education).* Center for Applied Research in Education, Inc., New York, 1965. 115 pp. AC 001 848

This is a general introduction to the field of university extension, i.e., those forms of university outreach which are usually administered by Cooperative or General Extension. Chapter I outlines the various types of extension programs and their historical origins. Separate chapters describe agricultural and general extension. Chapter IV reviews problems and issues in university extension and a final chapter discusses the future of extension and its relation to social change. Bibliography.

Sheats, Paul H. *The Case against the Adult Dropout.* CSLEA Occasional Papers, number 11. Center for the Study of Liberal Education for Adults, Boston, 1965. 16 pp.

Sheats urges federal legislation and support for programs of continuing technical, vocational, professional, and liberal adult education, accompanied by intensified efforts to enlist full adult participation. Pertinent surveys and educational endeavors are cited.

Sheldon, Henry D. "America's Adult in the Sixties; The Demographic Picture." In *Sociological Backgrounds of Adult Education,* edited by Hobert W. Burns, pp. 65–88. CSLEA Notes and Essays on Education for Adults, number 41. Center for the Study of Liberal Adult Education, Chicago, 1964.

Census data on various stages of adulthood (age 25 and over) are summarized according to overall age structure (1960 figures and 1970 estimates); sex composition; patterns of migration to cities and suburban areas; educational attainment; labor force participation; occupational distribution; income trends; marital status; and relationship and family status, including stages of parenthood. Increasing nonwhite migration to urban areas and the declining proportion of foreign-born Americans are noted.

Simons, Hans. *Higher Adult Education; Its Place and its Function.* CSLEA Notes and Essays on Education for Adults, number 26. Center for the Study of Liberal Education for Adults, Chicago, 1959. 14 pp.

A reflective essay defining higher adult education as a form of self-education in essential matters which form the mind to use intelligence for self-understanding and personality development in the individual. It is distinguished from the incidental matters common in adult education, from psychotherapy, and from the instruction and training which constitute most extension work. It is a voluntary activity of experienced persons, related to the circumstances of time and place, but not determined by them, a last refuge of liberal education, a manner of using leisure wisely. It introduces true individualization into the lives of adults whose formal education, often carried to the alumnus stage, has been focused on methodical socialization.

Southern Regional Education Board, Atlanta. "The Emerging City and Higher Adult Education." Papers presented at the Tulane University Institute for Deans and Directors of Adult Education (New Orleans, June 26–29, 1963) and at the Summer Graduate Workshop for Administrators of Higher Adult Education (University of Tennessee, July 22–August 10, 1963). 1963. 51 pp. AC 002 680

To meet the challenge of an increasingly urban population with more older members and more leisure time, higher adult education must concern itself with values, attitudes, and understanding as opposed to simple skills, facts, and information; new methods for deriving the objectives of such education must be developed. The higher adult education of the future should be liberal education so that adults may be increasingly equipped with skills of decision-making and public responsibility. Such education must include knowledge about the crucial and complex dilemmas and decisions confronting the citizen in the emerging cities. Increasing attention must be paid to programs in cultural and arts education. A major component of the developing programs must be education about the city, using the resources of the city and the city itself as the methods and materials. Administrators and programers must become increasingly concerned with widening their audiences so they involve not only the elite but also the man in the street. Adult educators have it within their power to turn changes in the emerging city into the means of enlarging their horizons and stimulating their imaginations.

Stern, Milton R. "Internal Relations." In his *People, Programs, and Persuasion: Some Remarks about Promoting University Adult Education.* CSLEA Notes and Essays, number 33, pp. 60–94. Center for the Study of Liberal Education for Adults, Chicago, 1961.

In a publication dealing, in general, with problems and techniques of recruitment and promotion in university adult education, section two focuses on the internal relations of the adult division with other parts of the university. Stern speaks in a reflective and cogent manner of the style or tone of voice the adult educator can use in taking positive action to improve relations with administration and faculty. He examines the self-conception of the adult educator and how he can increase understanding of his unique mission even in the midst of faculty prejudice, administrative indifference, and the other wearisome status problems which beset the adult education division of the university.

Taylor, Harold. "Adult Education in a Changing Society." In *Today and Tomorrow; Three Essays on Adult Education in the Future,* pp. 3–16. CSLEA Notes and Essays on Education for Adults, number 34. 1961.

Taylor suggests that the role of the university in American society is to enrich the lives of the citizens of all ages by introducing issues, questions, value judgments, knowledge, experience in the creative arts, political controversy, historical fact, and an understanding of the necessities and possibilities of a new society to students, citizens, and the community in which it exists. Emphasizes the philosophical changes occurring throughout the world, in developed, developing, and grossly underdeveloped regions alike. We in the United States must recognize that we are in the midst of a great search for a clear, national, liberal, democratic philosophy, consonant with the philosophies and goals of the world society. Education of the future will be a search for new meanings of contemporary thought in a realistic setting, and this will dictate new relationships between the community and the college (both undergraduate and adult).

Taylor, R. Robb, ed. *University and Community; Proceedings of a Conference (Wingspread, Racine, Wisconsin, April 25–26, 1963).* Association of Urban Universities, The Johnson Foundation, University of Wisconsin, Milwaukee, 1963. 147 pp.

Papers on various aspects of the relationship of the urban university to its community, with commentary and discussion by participants in a conference sponsored by the Association of Urban Universities and the Johnson Foundation. James Coke stresses the growing professionalization of all community agencies and recommends that the university cultivate this network of professionals and managers to carry teaching and research into the community. The university's role in research and development in industry is discussed by a panel of university representatives. Marvin Wachman explores the responsibilities of the university to the culturally deprived. David Popenoe discusses the emerging field of urban studies and the training needed for work in this field. J. Martin Klotsche takes up the use of social science research as an instrument for urban policy decision making.

Theobald, Robert. "Continuing Education; Key to the New Era." In *Perspective on Automation,* pp. 17–27. CSLEA Notes and Essays on Education for Adults, number 43. 1964.

In recent years there has been a growing conviction among social thinkers that increased emphasis on education is the key to the solution of problems of cybernation. Some guidelines for the study of a possible solution are: (1) the liberal education tradition will have to be reviewed; (2) with the coming of cybernation, any argument between advocates of strictly academic vs. informal nonacademic subjects is outdated; (3) a distinction must be made between information and knowledge; (4) with unlimited resources it is possible to educate the great majority of the population. We must recognize that our educational system is in the process of collapse and that we do not presently possess any policy for its resuscitation.

Thompson, Clarence H., ed. *Counseling the Adult Student.* Report of Commission 13 on Student Personnel Work for Adults in Higher Education. American College Personnel Association, 1967. 67 pp. ED 012 857

A preconvention workshop held by the American College Personnel Association in Dallas, Texas, March 17–18, 1967, dealt with the special characteristics and needs of adult participants, implications for counseling, recent progress and remaining areas of need in adult counseling, and the selection and training of personnel workers for adults in evening colleges. The main points were the following: (1) the distinctive life experiences, problems and obligations, physical and mental characteristics, and motives of adults call for experience-oriented teaching methods, special facilities, and a new approach to testing, admission, financial aid, and student activities; (2) acceptance of the individual, personal consistency and integrity, and understanding are essential counselor attributes; (3) the ultimate goal of counseling is to help the adult discover ways to realize his potential, respond more effectively to new experiences, and work out a meaningful, viable life style; (4) personnel trainees should be chosen primarily for appropriate character traits and academic background, and should receive broad training that stresses skills in short-term counseling. Proceedings included workshop evaluations. Document also contains appendixes, background statistical data, and 102 references.

Thornton, James W., Jr., and Wiley, John. *The Community Junior College,* 2d ed. New York, 1966. 300 pp.

In a general introductory volume on the junior college, Chapter 16 deals with continuing education in four sections: enrollment data, October, 1964, and extent of participation of private and public colleges; purposes of the part-time student; goals and objectives of the junior college in continuing education; issues in continuing education, centering on disagreement about scope of curriculum, academic standards, sources of support, problems of academic control of curriculum, and articulation with other educational agencies.

Tolley, William P. *American Universities in Transition and the New Role of Adult Education; Fourth Mansbridge Memorial Lecture (University of Leeds, June 16, 1966).* University of Leeds, England, 1967. 26 pp. AC 001 167

The modern university must advance knowledge, as well as conserve and transmit it. Growth of libraries, increases in graduate study, deeper involvement in the fine arts and in book publishing, international student exchange, federally sponsored research and instruction, and educational broadcasting are all dynamic trends in universities today, but the greatest is continuing education. Higher adult education has grown because of more leisure time, the paperback revolution, preparation for retirement, and the demand for new skills to meet rapid changes in business and industry. Such special collections as the Library for Continuing Education at Syracuse University reflect a rising concern for the special needs of nonresident, part-time, adult students. Expanded higher adult education will lead to a growth in university presses, sponsored research, international programs, and concern for metropolitan problems and urban extension.

Tyler, Ralph W. "An Evaluation of General Extension Work by Land-Grant Institutions." Paper presented to Centennial Convention of American Association of Land-Grant Colleges and State Universities, Nov. 14, 1961, Kansas City, Mo. 21 pp. AC 001 863

Assessing the work of general extension on the occasion of the Centennial Convention of the American Association of Land-Grant Colleges, Ralph Tyler reviews the growth of extension and summarizes results of a survey of extension programs and problems. He recommends such action directed to the problems as wide publicity to adult educational needs; demonstration programs actively involving key leaders in each state; publicity for successful programs; more financial support from federal, state, and local sources; more involvement of resident staff and leaders outside the university; designation of staff for program planning and development; cooperative preparation and procurement of learning materials; stimulation of commercial publishers to produce adult materials; cooperation in testing learning materials; definite budgeting for program development; and development of long-term planning for staff recruitment and training.

U.S. Civil Service Commission, Office of Career Development. *Executive Seminar Center, Kings Point.* 1963. 71 pp.

A proposed curriculum of 10 two-week courses for federal government careerists at grades GS-13 and above is described with attention to the purpose, scope, subject content, and scheduling of each. The suggested prerequisite course is Administration of Public Policy. The remaining courses deal with the economic, social, political, and diplomatic environment of federal operations; federal policy and the national economy; social needs and federal problems; implications of international conditions; effects of technological development; intergovernmental, i.e., joint federal, state and local problems and programs; administrative interrelationships (the need and the mechanics for coordinating programs and activities); and skills and goals of management. The potential audience, and costs and financial arrangements, are indicated. The annual budget estimate (fiscal year 1964) and the calendar and schedule for 1963–64 are included.

United Steelworkers of America, Pittsburgh, Department of Education. *An Experiment in Education.* 1960. 89 pp.

An account of the rationale and experience of the Steelworkers Institutes, perhaps the most successful, certainly the most durable, example of cooperation between a union and the universities which have operated the programs. The Institutes are summer residential experiences in a four-year sequence. The first year concentrates on the steelworker as he relates to his job and his role as a union member or leader; the second deals with his role as a citizen; the third takes up human relations and leadership training; and the unique fourth year is a pioneering effort at liberal education for labor.

Wedemeyer, Charles A., and Childs, Gayle B. *New Perspectives in University Correspondence Study.* Center for the Study of Liberal Education for Adults, Chicago, 1961. 78 pp. AC 001 052

Several million Americans are served by academic, private, and military correspondence programs, many of which employ group methods and mass media (radio, television, films). Correspondence programs can be adjusted to any background or level of ability, provide varied subject matter, permit study at any time or place, and meet academic and other needs through courses for college preparation or reinstatement, enrichment courses and similar advanced study, technical and professional education, and use with conferences and institutes. Group correspondence study in its several forms is conducive to economy, active discussion, student motivation, and immediate verbal practice, although special study guides, instructor orientation, and enrollment methods are usually required. Traditional correspondence methods have been combined by several universities in recent years with audiovisual media to provide explication and pacing and to improve motivation. Expanded provisions for secondary and higher education, topical courses, and liberal and humanistic studies are predicted, together with wider cooperation and international programs. Document includes tables (results of 2 evaluative surveys, and examples of TV-correspondence courses) and footnotes.

Whipple, James B. *Especially for Adults*. CSLEA Notes and Essays on Education for Adults, number 19. Center for the Study of Liberal Education for Adults, Chicago, 1957. 70 pp.

On the assumption that there are elements in adult education which make it different from collegiate education for youth and that these differences must be taken into account for effective teaching, Whipple reviews these differences in chapters devoted to nature and structure of adult experience, emotional states and thought patterns typical of adults, differences in adult time perspectives, and adult motivations.

White, Thurman. "The Emerging Curriculum." In *Growing Time*, pp. 59–62. CSLEA Notes and Essays on Education for Adults, number 44. 1964.

The adult curriculum is incomplete and discontinuous. Therefore, the adult cannot integrate his efforts to fulfill several learning concerns during any phase of maturity. There is a need to identify major themes of learning and develop a variety of programs to satisfy them. Major themes center around individual learning concerns and social concerns. Suggests that a counseling program for adults, using an integrated approach to program development, be used for developing five-year study plans for the adult students.

Wientge, King M., and Van Deursen, Malcolm. *Survey of Tuition Aid Plans of Business, Industry, and Government in Metropolitan St. Louis*. University College Research Publications, number 6. Washington University, St. Louis, University College, 1965. 28 pp.

This survey of 250 companies (of which 170 responded) is intended as an exploratory study of potential large-scale surveys of the St. Louis area.

Willie, Charles V. "Educating the Urban Student for the Urban Way of Life." In *Political Backgrounds of Adult Education; The University in Urban Society*, edited by Thomas Cummings, Jr. CSLEA Notes and Essays on Education for Adults, number 53. Center for the Study of Liberal Education for Adults, Boston, 1967. ED 011 367

The author deals with the role of the university in educating students to be citizens and leaders in our urbanized society. He sees urbanization as being different from, though related to, industrialization, and he sees distinct differences in the social and educational responses needed to deal with them. While industrialization, the main focus of our social and educational institutions, requires technological skills for work, urbanization requires the development of a sense of community. Willie believes that the university must seek to educate leaders from and for all levels of community—partly because all levels of community need leaders and partly because truth comes only from the fusion of a number of viewpoints—and that university education must become involved with current controversial community issues. The university must teach activists the benefits of reasoned thought and thinkers the methods and techniques of effective action. The author illustrates his discussion with a case study of school integration in Syracuse, N.Y., and 2 programs pertaining to community leadership development (the Thursday Breakfast Roundtable and the Community Action Training Center) sponsored by University College of Syracuse University.

Winters, Clifford L., Jr. "The New and Challenging Role of Counseling and Guidance." In *Counseling and Guidance in the Evening College; Proceedings of the Annual Meeting of the Association of University Evening Colleges (23rd, 1961)*, pp. 49–56.

Essay proposes comprehensive evening college counseling centers providing professional counselors to meet the personal and career needs of adult students and incorporating auxiliary administrative services. Physical resources, program planning, publicity, student-faculty relations, and community services are viewed as necessary supporting elements.

Wisconsin, University of, Madison, University Extension Division. *School for Workers 35th Anniversary Papers; Early Labor Studies at Wisconsin: Wisconsin and Workers' Education; Problems and Prospects in Labor Education*. 1960. 101 pp.

A symposium on the occasion of the thirty-fifth anniversary of the Wisconsin School for Workers. Several papers deal with the history of the school and the influence of John R. Commons and Selig Perlman. Joseph Mire reviews recent trends in labor programs. Emery Bacon and Brendan Sexton discuss excellence in labor education; Jack London develops principles for labor education and reviews problems of staffing and evaluation.

AMERICAN COUNCIL ON EDUCATION

LOGAN WILSON, *President*

The American Council on Education, founded in 1918, is a *council* of educational organizations and institutions. Its purpose is to advance education and educational methods through comprehensive voluntary and cooperative action on the part of American educational associations, organizations, and institutions.